Technology and Inequality

Jonathan P. Allen

Technology and Inequality

Concentrated Wealth in a Digital World

Jonathan P. Allen
School of Management
University of San Francisco
San Francisco, CA
USA

ISBN 978-3-319-56957-4   ISBN 978-3-319-56958-1   (eBook)
DOI 10.1007/978-3-319-56958-1

Library of Congress Control Number: 2017939558

© The Editor(s) (if applicable) and The Author(s) 2017
This work is subject to copyright. All rights are solely and exclusively licensed by the Publisher, whether the whole or part of the material is concerned, specifically the rights of translation, reprinting, reuse of illustrations, recitation, broadcasting, reproduction on microfilms or in any other physical way, and transmission or information storage and retrieval, electronic adaptation, computer software, or by similar or dissimilar methodology now known or hereafter developed.
The use of general descriptive names, registered names, trademarks, service marks, etc. in this publication does not imply, even in the absence of a specific statement, that such names are exempt from the relevant protective laws and regulations and therefore free for general use.
The publisher, the authors and the editors are safe to assume that the advice and information in this book are believed to be true and accurate at the date of publication. Neither the publisher nor the authors or the editors give a warranty, express or implied, with respect to the material contained herein or for any errors or omissions that may have been made. The publisher remains neutral with regard to jurisdictional claims in published maps and institutional affiliations.

Cover credit: Pattern adapted from an Indian cotton print produced in the 19th century

Printed on acid-free paper

This Palgrave Macmillan imprint is published by Springer Nature
The registered company is Springer International Publishing AG
The registered company address is: Gewerbestrasse 11, 6330 Cham, Switzerland

PREFACE

Rising inequality has become a key issue for researchers, policy makers, and the public, but the influence of technology on inequality is still open for debate. What role does digital technology play in inequality? Is technology one of the best hopes for creating widespread opportunity? Or is the digital world being used to reinforce existing concentrations of wealth and power?

In this book, we examine the relationship between technology and inequality, seeking new ways to analyze this relationship, with an emphasis on the business practices surrounding technology. This book explores how technology creates wealth, and how this wealth is captured and shared in economies that are increasingly digitally mediated.

We also investigate how the business practices of technology companies relate to larger transformations in wealth and power. Over the past 40 years, as economic inequality has risen in the developed world, wealth has shifted from real to financial assets, and from the energy and commodities sectors to the virtual economy of information technology and finance. The largest digital technology companies have played a direct role in this wealth shift, creating trillions of dollars of equity and profit. The largest technology companies have become extremely capable value creators and value capturers, through their historically unprecedented abilities to experiment, collect exclusive data, and scale.

We examine three detailed case studies—the search industry, the social media industry, and the more recent 'sharing' economy movement—for evidence of the relationship between technology and inequality over the past few decades. The ability to test and improve new business models is an important part of the technology and inequality story, especially if the wealth created through technology remains highly concentrated.

In the end, we hope to find new ideas for restoring technology to its rightful place as an 'engine of opportunity,' as a source of widespread empowerment and social mobility rather than a means for further concentrating wealth and power.

San Francisco, USA   Jonathan P. Allen

Acknowledgements

My favorite spouse, Sharon, has made the journey all the way from college to the Outer Richmond. Thanks for your love and patience sweetie.

My intellectual sparring partner and teacher, Todd Sayre, has better equipped me to take on the big questions in business, and in life.

Many supported me during the writing process and sabbatical travels. The Sebastopol Allens (Mark, Michelle, Remy, and Quincy) kept me pampered and emotionally stable. Rachel Brem and Jack Schonbrun facilitated many East Bay writing and feasting days. Séamas and Louise Kelly, Urszula and Thomas Grassl, Brad Schmidt, and Fabienne Grandamy took care of us in Europe. Cathy Ching, Richard Streat, and Zachary Streat sheltered us in London. Gary Ching and Zachary Burns helped greatly with the practicalities of life during the long birthing process.

This book benefitted from seminars at the University of Manchester, thanks to Delia Vasquez, and the University of Hertfordshire, thanks to Jyoti Choudrie.

I owe a debt to the many who have helped me traverse the interdisciplinary wilderness of technology, business, and society. What began with my unusual yet delightful upbringing (Mom and Glenn's move overseas, Dad's international trips, and Grandpa's exotic library destroyed by Katrina) continued through UC Santa Cruz, the CORPS program at UC Irvine, and was furthered by many genius colleagues and beverage consumption partners at Cambridge, Purdue, and now the University of San Francisco. In the unlikely event of fame and fortune, please feel free to claim a share.

Sabbatical support from the School of Management, University of San Francisco is gratefully acknowledged. Nicole Mauro provided much needed editorial help.

Finally, thanks to Casio, Tandy, Commodore, Sinclair, Atari, Palm, and Apple for all the good times!

Contents

1 Why Is Inequality Increasing in a Digital World?   1

2 Information Technology and Wealth Concentration   25

3 The Digital Economy: New Markets, New Gatekeepers   43

4 Regulation and Taxation: The New Digital Advantage   61

5 Models, Mediation, and Mobilization: A Framework for Analyzing Technology and Inequality   77

6 Technology and Inequality Case Study: Search   93

7 Technology and Inequality Case Study: Social Media   107

8 Technology and Inequality Case Study: The Sharing Economy   121

9 Restoring Technology as an Engine of Opportunity   137

Index   155

List of Figures

Fig. 1.1 Income share to top 1% of households, United States, 1913–2015 (World Wealth & Income Database 2017) — 8

Fig. 1.2 Productivity and real median family income growth, United States, 1948–2013 (Economic Policy Institute 2017) — 9

Fig. 2.1 *IEA* savings, money market, CD, interest checking; *other assets* vehicles, rental properties, business, unsecured liabilities, other. — 26

Fig. 2.2 Market capitalization of S&P 500 by sector type, United States, 1980–2015 (Standard and Poor's 2017) — 28

Fig. 5.1 The conceptual framework: business model, mediation, mobilization, and wealth effects — 78

CHAPTER 1

Why Is Inequality Increasing in a Digital World?

Abstract This chapter reviews arguments about the relationship between technology and inequality, the evidence for rising inequality in the most technologically advanced economies, and why rising inequality in a digital world is surprising. It presents two main schools of thought about the relationship—the 'technological' school, and the 'institutional context' school. Finally, it proposes identifying new mechanisms for restoring technology as an engine of opportunity.

Keywords Technology · Wealth inequality · Eras of technology · Institutional context · Opportunity

Why is inequality increasing in a more digital world? What do we know about the relationship between technology and inequality? Are there ways of thinking about this relationship that open up new possibilities for restoring technology as an engine of greater opportunity rather than greater inequality? These are the questions we seek to answer, incorporating arguments from economic, social, business, and technology literatures.

Two major schools of thought dominate discussions about technology and inequality: the 'technological' school that focuses on how digital technology leads to globalization, automation, and changing demand for skills; and the 'institutional context' school that focuses on the economic rules of the game affecting inequality, such as taxation, regulation, and corporate governance, with technology playing a supporting or background role. Each school corresponds to one of the basic philosophical positions used in the analysis of technology: technology as 'force,' or an independent cause of change humanity reacts to; and technology as 'tool' or an instrument that reflects and implements human choices.

The main aspect of inequality we focus on is wealth inequality, which is even more unevenly distributed than income. Private wealth in the US economy has shifted dramatically since 1980, moving away from real assets toward financial ones, and away from the energy and materials sectors to the virtualized economy of information technology and finance.

This virtualized economy affects not only what is produced and consumed, it also affects the very operation and regulation of markets themselves. Technologically mediated markets are different than traditional 'free' markets due to significant information asymmetries, non-transparent algorithms, and winner-take-all effects. These differences are not accidental or temporary deviations from traditional markets, but are, instead, the 'new normal.' An analysis of specific technology mediation choices, combined with particular business model decisions, offers a new way of examining shifts in wealth and power.

The 'institutional context' school highlights regulatory and legal issues, both of which have become important mechanisms driving wealth inequality in the technology sector. Technology companies are highly proficient in creating business structures that avoid taxation through the use of intellectual property law and global regulatory arbitrage. The technology sector has also developed strong relationships with national and local governments, as seen in the case of the 'sharing economy' which is dependent on regulatory change to survive. Technology companies are able to motivate and mobilize a variety of actors to participate in new ways of doing business, and maintain their participation with just the right level of inducements. Technology companies learn how to improve their business models through constant experimentation and access to unique data. For this reason, studying the business practices that keep multiple parties working together is another useful tool for analyzing the technology and inequality relationship.

Analyzing the effects of technology on any aspect of the world, including inequality, requires conceptual tools and an awareness of our underlying assumptions about technology. The rich tradition of science and technology studies (STS), along with the history and philosophy of technology, are fields of study that provide us with a set of concepts that analyze technology as a 'force,' a 'tool,' and many other variations of the two.

We borrow from this rich tradition to create a simple four-part conceptual framework. For each case of technology and inequality, we analyze how *mediation, model, mobilization,* and *wealth effects* evolve over time. Digital *mediation* is the set of specific technology choices used to represent aspects of the world, and to represent relationships between things in the world. The business *model* is the definition and implementation of how technology creates and captures economic value. *Mobilization* is the set of techniques used to keep different groups participating in a digital business model. And *wealth effects* are the changes in wealth distribution that result from specific *mediation, model,* and *mobilization* choices over time.

By focusing on technology choices and business practices, we hope to find new insights into inequality that bring together the technological and the institutional context schools.

1.1 The Computing Revolution and Expectations of Empowerment

Questions about how technology affects the world are rooted in expectations about what technology can and should do. Digital technology has already passed through at least four eras, each era being defined by different cultural expectations and technology role models. The four periods identified by Elliott and Kraemer (2008) are the Mainframe era, the Personal Computing era, the Networking era of the Internet, and the Ubiquitous Computing era of mobile devices and networks. We might be moving into a fifth era of cultural understanding based on artificial intelligence and massive data sets, but that remains to be seen.

Our expectations about how technology and inequality are related differ, depending on which picture of digital technology we are most influenced by. For example, I came of age in the Personal Computing era before the Internet was widespread. In contrast to the Mainframe era before it, the vision of the PC era was to make computing power more widely available, and so many of my expectations of technology are associated with empowerment and opportunity.

As a teenager first falling in love with computer technology in the 1980s, I would have been pleasantly surprised by the growth in computing power over the next 30 years, and how much information capability would be put in the hands of billions of people. It would have been hard to imagine a day, as I played my pixelated games on early Commodores, Sinclairs, and Apples with cassette tape drives, when every student would carry the equivalent of a supercomputer not just in their backpacks, but in their pockets as well. I certainly had no awareness back then of a largely open, non-commercial, global networking technology that would eventually connect over 50% of the world's population, the Internet. It would have been equally hard to imagine fiber optic connections to homes and apartments, or personal data storage measured in the billions or trillions of characters available in a global 'cloud' for a few dollars a month. The technological joys I experienced were simple ones, satisfying typical teenage desires like having fun, exploring, challenging myself, and knowing more than the adults.

As the character of digital technology evolved from its roots in the Mainframe era for government agencies and large corporations to the Personal Computer and Internet eras of the 1980s and 1990s, many attempted to predict what this technological shift might mean for society.[1] For those of us brought up in the Personal Computer era, it seemed reasonable to believe that vast increases in individual computing power, combined with widespread access to global networks, might increase opportunity, empower individuals, and perhaps even decentralize political, organizational, and economic power. Digital technology might even make the world more environmentally sustainable by making information about eco-efficiency more widely available, and by replacing resource-intensive physical products with digital ones.

Predicting the social impacts of technology based on its essential features or capabilities is a common form of reasoning known as 'technological determinism.' The optimistic variant of determinism, known as 'technological utopianism,' (Kling 1996) argues that a technological capability inevitably leads to a positive social change without significant negative side effects on other parts of society. Its close cousin, 'technological dystopianism,' uses the same logic, but, instead, argues for a social change that is relentlessly negative.

Technological determinism arguments offer a clear, simple story of causality that is easy to explain and test. As critics of technological determinism have shown, however, deterministic arguments make strong assumptions about how technology is created and used in exactly the same way, in every situation (Smith and Marx 1994). For purely deterministic arguments to apply, technology has to be designed and implemented in a consistent way unaffected by human choice. Using technological determinism as an analytic tool requires the analyst to separate technology from society in order to make it an independent causal agent. Determinism also reduces multifaceted technologies to a single function or capability. While this simplification of reality can be a useful analytic starting point, technology in practice always seems to be a fascinating interplay between the natural world beyond our control and the human world of action and decision. The debate over the best way to understand technology's relationship to society will be something we return to many times over the course of our investigation.

Expectations of the Personal Computing revolution of the 1980s have been linked to the wider social upheavals and the counterculture of the 1960s and 1970s (Markoff 2005). The early homebrew computer clubs and the hacker ethos valued sharing and openness (Levy 2001). The PC era brought with it expectations that computing power would augment human intellect and reform education. Connected together, PCs would lead to a more informed and engaged electorate, invigorating the democratic process.

At the same time, the PC era celebrated the commercial possibilities of technology, creating visions of young entrepreneurs launching companies from Silicon Valley garages, outmaneuvering giant corporations and making themselves rich in the process. In contrast with the Mainframe era, dominated by large corporations such as IBM, the PC era saw feisty startups backed by 'angel' investors and venture capital. Superstars such as Bill Gates, the teen hacker from a wealthy background, became cultural icons of business success while simultaneously appearing revolutionary. New fortunes were created, and power was put in the hands of everyday people.

The opening of the Internet to the public in the 1990s reinforced the notion of technology as popular empowerment. The ethos of sharing through open standards and freely available open source software felt victorious, with Internet technology around the world winning over its closed and proprietary competitors. Here was a technology not controlled by any particular government or corporation, but, instead, by volunteers and international associations collaborating for the common good.

During the Mainframe era, the primary social concern was automation displacing human jobs. The Personal Computing era brought speculation about how widespread computing could improve education and empower people politically through a better-informed populace and better tools for political organizing. The Internet era saw more specific predictions about how computing would interact with wealth, income, and economic power.

Building on the idea of greater democratization, the Internet was seen as a mechanism to create a more ideal, fully informed, and perfectly competitive market (Bakos 1998). In the language of transaction cost economics, there is a fundamental choice between organizing collective activity through a market or within an organizational hierarchy. The superior informing capability of the Internet was predicted to lead to more use of markets as opposed to large companies. This choice became intertwined with value-laden notions of the moral superiority of free markets, with its voluntary actions and fully informed participants, versus hierarchies based on command and control.

The Internet's ability to share information formed the basis of a deterministic argument that technology would make economic markets function more effectively. In the Networking era, perfect information transparency would make searching easier, promoting a positive cycle of more competition, efficiency, and consumer choice. This concept acquired a name, the 'new economy,'[2] and led to a massive wealth shift into the technology sector during the dot.com era of the late 1990s.

The expectations of technology-induced perfect markets and perfect competition that arose from the Networking era made specific assumptions about how information would be created, controlled, and shared. The Internet would bring about greater disintermediation, directly connecting producers and consumers. For example, travel agents would be replaced by consumers buying their own airline tickets online. The possibility of complex re-intermediation through technology, where market participants would only see certain kinds of information revealed by technologies, such as search engines or social media, was not yet apparent.

In the current Ubiquitous era, the importance of mobile devices and constant connectivity has shifted expectations toward human communication and interaction. In today's technology debates, expectations of personal empowerment and enrichment are not as discussed as the effects of social media interactions, or government surveillance. Economic expectations subsided as the industry fought to recover from the dot.com bust of the early 2000s, and it was only after the economic crisis in 2007–2008 that expectations of technology started to include associations with inequality. Increasing economic inequality in the developed world became a highly visible issue, and the search for explanations began. Many of those explanations included digital technology, though only some prioritized technology as a key driver.

Like many predictions about the future, predictions about the impact of technology tend to say more about the period in which the predictions were made than about the future, reflecting the concerns and anxieties of their times. For the earliest machines, huge, impersonal, and used only by the largest government agencies and institutions, automation was the primary concern. The PC revolution brought possibilities of empowerment, and the Internet, or Networking era, brought new speculations about economic empowerment and decentralization. Whatever technology is current at the time shapes social concerns, forever raising new questions. For example, globalization and environmental impact only arose when those became broader societal and political issues. Today's new technological environment, highly mobile, social, and infused with massive databases, intersects with new societal issues such as inequality.

It is important to remember that the different eras of digital technology are not mutually exclusive, because older and newer technology types co-exist at any specific moment. The eras of cultural expectations overlap, creating a complex jumble of framings that make it challenging to talk about any single thing that technology does, even if one accepts the simplifications of technology determinism, yet few would deny the important role technology has played, and will continue to play, in building the world, for good or ill.

In a world of widespread computing power, especially after the Personal Computing and Internet eras, predictions about the impact of technology varied. Overall, we can say that once we left the Mainframe era, few predicted that economic and political power might become more concentrated with the rise of digital technology, and fewer still wondered why a digital world be a more unequal one.

1.2 What We Know About Inequality

After the financial crisis of 2007–2008, concern about severe economic inequality expanded from a narrow academic debate to a larger political issue. From mainstream organizations representing the wealthiest and most powerful elements of society, such as the World Economic Forum, to organizations representing the poorest and most vulnerable, such as Oxfam, severe income inequality was declared one of the most significant global risks to humanity's future[3]. The Occupy movement politicized the divide between the top 1% of income earners, whose incomes were increasing, and the 99%, whose incomes were not (Van Gelder 2011).

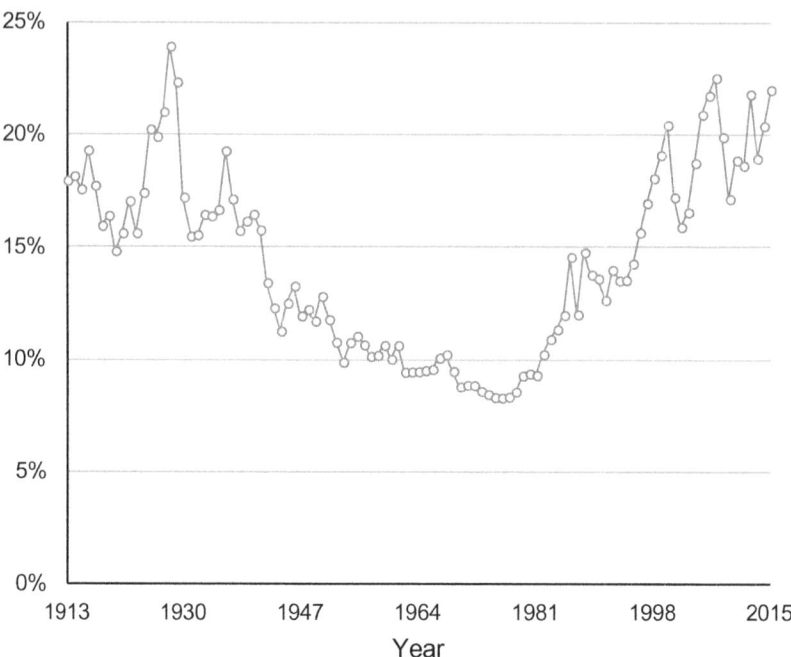

Fig. 1.1 Income share to top 1% of households, United States, 1913–2015 (World Wealth & Income Database 2017)

The academic work on income inequality by Piketty, Saez, and colleagues reached a wider audience.[4] By examining tax records in the US and western Europe over many decades, Piketty characterized the twentieth century as a story of high and increasing economic inequality through the 1920s, reduced inequality after World War II through the 1950s and 1960s, and then increasing inequality from 1980 on, returning in the present day almost to its peak in the 1920s.[5]

These findings were echoed by the US Census Bureau.[6] Since 1980, median household income remained almost the same, while the top 1% of households captured most of the income gains in the following three decades (see Fig. 1.1). Overall productivity in the US economy continued to increase (Sprague 2014), but only the top 1% of households in terms of income were capturing the economic gains (as seen in Fig. 1.2).

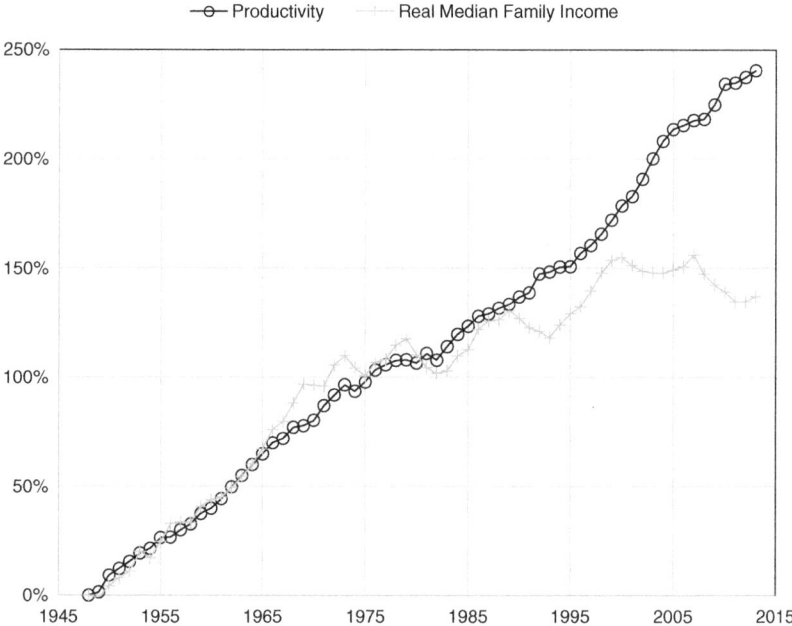

Fig. 1.2 Productivity and real median family income growth, United States, 1948–2013 (Economic Policy Institute 2017)

Since then, income inequality has been on the rise across all of the developed economies, not just the United States (Cingano 2014).

Though rising inequality in developed economies had been a long-term trend for decades, Piketty argued that academic work on inequality was slow to reach mainstream acceptance because of ideological reasons. During the cold war period, according to Piketty, Western nations sought to prove the superiority of capitalism as an economic system. One of the best forms of evidence for capitalism's superiority over the Soviet socialist economies was a healthy and growing middle class. Early economic inequality researchers, led by Kuznets, correctly identified economic inequality as decreasing during this 'golden age' after World War II, and used this early data to prove the superiority of their preferred economic system. Overturning a belief in the power of the western economic system to create a healthy middle class would require not just a re-examination of data, according to this argument, but a re-examination of fundamental assumptions.

Even though the new school of inequality research highlighted the widening gap between 1 and 99%, researchers also found growing differences between the top and the very top. Within the top 1% of households, the top 0.1%, and even the top 0.01%, captured a disproportionate share of the income gains. These superclasses of income earners included CEOs, financiers, lawyers, and some entertainers.

Economic research focused on income inequality rather than wealth inequality, but wealth is even more unequally distributed than income. According to Oxfam, global wealth inequality has become so severe that only eight people have as much wealth as the poorest 3.6 billion people, or half of all humanity. Wealth and income are, of course, related. As Piketty argued, wealth represents the 'power of the past.' In his theory, if the investment returns on existing wealth surpass the overall growth rate of the economy, an economic system will tend to concentrate wealth in the hands of the already wealthy, which is the situation we in the developed world find ourselves in today.

There is a broad academic consensus today that income and wealth inequality are increasing in developed economies, particularly in the United States, though there remains something of a political debate over the degree to which economic inequality is a problem. Stiglitz and others provide an economic answer, asserting the 'price of inequality' is reduced economic growth (Stiglitz 2012). Economies become distorted by too much wealth in too few hands, where it does not create sufficient demand and is invested in luxury goods and other less productive activities. Researchers outside of economics argue that greater income inequality is correlated with negative social outcomes, such as increased crime and worse health, independent of absolute wealth level.[7] On the other side is an economic theory that inequalities provide incentives, rewarding those who contribute the most to the economy.

But what level of economic inequality is severe enough to be a problem? One way to assess the importance of inequality is to define the purpose of an economic system. If defining economic purpose as human development, severe inequality is then a problem to the extent that the economy fails to serve people's basic needs. Sen's classic definition of economic development argues the purpose of an economy is to give people the resources they need to achieve practical freedom, or the ability to make choices about how they want to live (Sen 1999). Severe inequality is problematic to the extent that it deprives people of access to the basic resources needed to have choices in life.

Changes in economic inequality in the developing world have been more mixed over the past 40 years. Rising wealth in economies such as China have lowered rates of absolute poverty in the world while somewhat reducing economic inequality between countries (Ravallion 2014). However, income inequality within developing nations has been rising in many cases, and income growth in whole regions of the world is not keeping pace. One of the great hopes of technology-based economic development was that by leapfrogging to the latest technologies, such as mobile networks, the developing world would have a quicker path to economic development, however, digital technologies such as fiber optic infrastructure, along with the skills and resources needed to use them, have not spread as evenly as some predicted a few decades ago. Fiber optic connections and computing power are unequally distributed internationally, even more highly than income or wealth as measured by Gini coefficients (Hilbert 2014). Even with the global adoption of the Internet and mobile devices, there is still talk of an international digital divide, and technology for development continues to be an important research topic.

Forms of inequality other than wealth and income persist, though whether and to what extent these inequalities have intensified over the past 40 years is not as well understood as income and wealth inequality. Evidence exists that gender and ethnic inequality live on in the digital age, such as the persistent wage gap between men and women, but the evidence is not as clear that these forms of inequality have actually increased in the digital era in the same way as economic inequality.

Inequalities such as gender and ethnicity enter the technology discussion through debates about technology education, and subsequent employment. Enrollment in technology subjects, such as computer science, is still among the most gender biased in secondary schools and universities (Sax et al. 2016), and technical educational opportunities in the United States are fewer in lower income schools with higher ethnic minority representation[8] in part because underexposure to computer science topics early in education leads to fewer computer science majors in universities.

Once students enter the workforce, the world of technology investors, engineers, and managers is not equally represented by all genders and ethnic backgrounds. According to their own diversity hiring reports, large Silicon Valley firms have not yet made much progress in reducing ethnic and gender disparities (Rodriguez 2016). Technology firms argue that the 'pipeline' of female and minority talent is the barrier preventing them from addressing these inequalities. However, a lack of diversity persists even in managerial and other non-technology-related jobs in technology companies (USA Today 2016). On the investor side, there are few women and ethnic minorities in decision-making roles at venture capital firms (National Venture Capital Association 2016).

Discussions about gender and ethnic inequality intersect with economic inequality, particularly in the United States, through the support and resources families give to their children for their education. There are substantial ethnic inequalities between household assets in the US, with the median white household having 10 times the net worth of black and Hispanic households (Kochhar and Fry 2014), and the majority of US households have either very little or no savings whatsoever (Huddleston 2016). Wealth disparities have not decreased in recent decades. In the aftermath of the 2007–2008 financial crisis, the wealth of ethnic minority households was more concentrated in real estate, which collapsed more drastically than financial assets, and took longer to recover.

While all types of inequality cannot be reduced to economic inequality, enough connections exist to make economic income or wealth a reasonable area to focus on when taking on questions about technology and inequality. Economic wealth creation around the world, as measured by per capita GDP, correlates closely with broader measures of welfare such as health and leisure time (Jones and Klenow 2016), supporting our choice of economic inequality, and, in particular, wealth inequality, as a useful means for investigating technology and inequality more broadly.

Overall, our understanding of economic inequality is that, after decades of reduced inequality from the 1940s to the 1970s in the developed world, wealth and income inequality increased from the 1980s on, most significantly in the US, but across the developed world as well. The picture in the developing world has been more mixed, but global wealth inequality still exists on an unprecedented scale. Severe economic inequality is a problem to the extent that it impedes widespread human development, the ultimate purpose of human economies. Other forms of inequality, such as gender and ethnicity, appear to be resilient in the digital age, especially as they relate to income, wealth, and the education and health disparities that continue to exist.

1.3 Explaining Inequality: Technology and Institutional Context

While the empirical reality of greater income and wealth inequality in the developed world since 1980 is mostly agreed upon, there are a variety of explanations as to why it exists. Many of the stories of increasing inequality argue that technology plays a role, but they differ in how important technology is for understanding rising inequality.

As a starting point, we contrast two main schools of explanation. The first is the 'technological' school that centers information technology at the heart of the inequality story. The second school, which we call 'institutional context,' places other contextual factors before technology, with technology serving more as a 'tool' to capture wealth and advance specific interests. It is too strong to say these two schools are conflicting and mutually exclusive views, though debates do occasionally break out, as when Stiglitz derides the 'technological optimists' for their belief that the dislocations created by technology will always correct themselves, and new jobs will always appear to absorb labor displaced by automation. It is more accurate to say the two schools of explanation differ in emphasis. The list of overall factors and forces is often the same, but the main causal agent changes.

The technological school focuses on attributes of the technology that have a social impact, using the logic of technological determinism. The most prominent explanation used by the technological school is the change in demand for work skills brought about by digital processing, storage, and sharing. There is extensive economics literature on skills-biased technological change[9] (SBTC) suggesting that as the demand for skills changes in the digital world, and even between different technological eras, people equipped with these new skills are able to capture more income and wealth from the overall economy.

With digital technology, the new skills required either consist of general abstract thought, including analysis and symbolic manipulation, or specific STEM (Science, Technology, Engineering, and Mathematics) skills directly relating to the design and use of technology. Reich's original theory argued that the nature of work as a whole was changing, with technology and globalization rewarding the abstract work of 'symbolic analysts' disproportionately to other traditional forms of work (Reich 1991). Or, perhaps, the total amount of work that needs to be done is being reduced. If new technology makes work less necessary, then society faces the possibility of increased leisure, or increased exploitation of a pool of workers who can no longer find a job (Mason 2016). Physical labor might remain, but an entire mass of semi-skilled work involving simple decisions and information transfer could be replaced either with technology, or cheaper labor overseas.

The data from Goldin and Katz, among many others, confirms that higher education continues to be associated with higher income, and the income gap between the more and less educated has continued to increase in recent decades. The technological school attributes this income premium from higher education to the rise of digital technology.

The skills-biased technological change argument echoes fear from the first digital age, the Mainframe era, that automation would lead to job loss. Commentators that focus on attributes of the new technology, such as Brynjolfsson and McAfee (2014), point to the long history of predictions that automation will lead to job losses, arguing that these predictions have always been wrong in the past. They also point out, however, that there is no particular theoretical reason why replacement jobs have always appeared for those automated out of the labor market, a pattern that may or may not continue.

Changing demand for worker skills, rewarding either general analytic ability or specific STEM skills, is not the only way that technology could affect inequality. The attributes of digital technology could favor 'superstars' at the expense of everyone else. According to the superstar argument, new technology amplifies the skills of a single best person or group (Brynjolfsson et al. 2010). Because the marginal cost of copies is low, or even zero, in the digital era, and global access to information is cheap, consumers will always choose to see the best TV show, the best doctor, or the best performance of any kind if given the option, leaving little or nothing for the rest.

It is not just the cost of copying information that can lead to 'superstar' effects, but the power and reach of software as well. Attributes of the technology seem to amplify the skills of individual superstar programmers and designers. Studies of programmers suggest that the best are perhaps two times, five times, or even 10 times more productive than average ones (Weinberg 1998), a larger productivity variation than found in typical office or factory work. Software and networks might also extend the reach of particular management decisions and policies made by a few superstars, through the ability to encode a decision in software and implement it quickly across an entire organization (Scott Morton

1991). If a skilled performance could be partially or completely captured in software, for example in a medical diagnosis or a tax return, the skills of a few superstar doctors or lawyers would become more valuable relative to an average performer that could be partially or completely replaced. The superstar argument relies on technological determinism, so its validity depends on assuming that the technology will always provide a clearly better alternative in every situation.

Related to the superstar argument is the 'winner-take-all' argument, which focuses on the network effects of digital technology. For many digital technologies, the value of using a technology increases with the number of other users. This is most obviously the case for communication and social media technologies, but it can also be true for widely used software that benefits from complements or add-ons, such as apps that make mobile devices more valuable. The more people who use an operating system like Microsoft Windows or Google's Android, the bigger an audience to attract the developers who will create a better pool of software applications. The winner-take-all effect increases inequality by concentrating wealth in the hands of one technology provider, or a few, and so we find ourselves in a world of just one, or perhaps two, competing massive technology platforms in many technology areas, for example social media, personal computers, mobile devices, and, increasingly, online shopping.

The other school of thought, which we call 'institutional context,' places technology in the background. Technology often plays a role, but usually as a means to take advantage of some other economic or political opportunity. The institutional context school argues inequality is increasing because the rules of the economic game have been written (or rewritten) in favor of the wealthy and powerful (Reich 2016). But what are these rules? They include, most notably, taxation and government subsidies, but also include other structural rules, such as the details of intellectual property laws, bankruptcy laws, monopoly regulation and enforcement, financial regulations, and all the other rules of the economic game that determine how economic gains are created and distributed. Their arguments highlight the idea that real economic markets are more complex than the free market ideal of minimal regulation and perfect information. A highly complicated set of rules gives the wealthy and powerful ample opportunity to exploit complexity in ways that those with fewer resources cannot, and to rewrite the rules in their favor through political connections.

In the institutional context arguments, technology interacts with the economic rules of the game in ways that make a difference for inequality. Digital technology offers opportunities to rewrite the rules—or deliberately not rewrite the rules as conditions change. For example, traditional monopoly regulations might have to be modified to account for the concentrating power of network effects and winner-take-all, but regulators may decline to adapt old regulations to new situations, or refuse to enforce them altogether. Another example are new regulations that lead to the decline of unionized labor, which is associated with higher inequality due to the equalizing effects of unionization on wage distribution, particularly for jobs that are semi-skilled (Card et al. 2004). Digital technology could act as a tool in a deliberate strategy to reduce the power of unionized labor, for example by enabling substitute labor overseas.

The gray areas of regulations between nations offer rich possibilities for creating complex rules and structures that would disproportionately benefit the already wealthy and powerful. Technology companies have become especially skilled at exploiting differences in international regulations to avoid taxation. Estimates vary, but the largest US corporations have amassed an unprecedented amount of cash, on the order of $3–5 trillion US dollars, with over half of that cash being kept overseas (Moody's Investor Service 2016). Five of the top 10 companies on the list of overseas holdings are from the digital technology sector, with Apple being the largest (Citizens for Tax Justice 2016).

Other types of companies can benefit from complex international tax avoidance structures, but technology companies have the special advantage of using intellectual property rules to shift profits to subsidiaries in jurisdictions with near-zero tax rates and minimal regulatory oversight. Companies whose wealth can be defined as intellectual assets can assign ownership of those assets to a subsidiary anywhere in the world, then make payments to that subsidiary for the use of their intellectual assets. No physical transactions need to take place, thanks to the power of digital technology. Apple's Ireland subsidiary is a classic example. The European Union estimates that Apple Ireland paid an effective tax rate of less than 0.01% on over $100 billion in profits (European Commission 2016). Following the arguments of Piketty and others of the institutional context school, taxation rates are probably the most important mechanism for changing income inequality.

The line between the technological and institutional context schools can be blurry. There are few voices in the debate claiming that technology plays absolutely no role in inequality, though Stiglitz perhaps comes closest, arguing that technology cannot be the cause because inequality has increased more in some countries than others, yet each developed economy has access to roughly the same digital technology. He uses the same argument to criticize the skills-biased technological change research, arguing the same skill changes across different countries would lead to equal changes in inequality. That leaves differences in 'institutional context' as the primary explanation of different levels of inequality in different countries. One counter argument would be that technology access and use across the developed world may not be exactly the same. Even basic technology infrastructure factors, such as the extent of high-speed Internet access, still vary among developed nations.

The technological school arguments tend not to engage directly with the issues brought up by their institutional context counterparts. The assumptions of technological determinism in these arguments can be strong, and largely unexamined. Debates within the technological school focus more on the size and significance of phenomena such as skills-biased technological change and 'superstar' effects, rather than competing explanations from the institutional context. In today's debates about inequality, there is little conversation or engagement between the two schools, and we are very far from directly testing one set of explanations versus another, so explanations that incorporate both sides of this divide are not as examined as they should be.

1.4 Restoring Technology-Driven Opportunity

After examining how technology and inequality are related, our goal for this book is to think about normative future steps, what ought to be done. Assuming that severe inequality is undesirable, mostly because of its negative consequences for human development, we should use this investigation to find new ways of making technology an engine of widespread opportunity—or, to at least stop digital technology from becoming a mechanism for increasing inequality. Those of us brought up in the Personal Computing or Networking eras were expecting a digital world to empower and enrich people as a whole, not further concentrate wealth within a global elite.

Both the technological and institutional context schools have settled into familiar sets of remedies for increased inequality. For the technological school, to the extent that economic inequality is a problem, better education is the main solution. Focusing on the skills-biased technological change argument, more education and higher skill levels are the best hope to 'win the race' against technological change. The technological school often sees skill changes as an opportunity to move people into more meaningful and better paid work, with its greatest optimists pointing to times in the past when technological change generated enough new jobs to replace the ones made obsolete.

The sheer power of digital technology is enough to give many hopes for the future, even if previous exponential increases in digital capability have arrived during our current period of rising inequality. The power of automation can be used to remove drudgery and launch a period of mass leisure. Brynjofsson and McAfee argue that tremendous leaps in new era technologies, such as artificial intelligence and big data, could serve all of humanity. The breathtaking speed at which technical power has increased gives these optimists hope, even if the technology is deployed mostly by large corporations and institutions. Digital technology further liberates us from the physical world, reducing the amount of material resources needed to make things and decreasing our burden on the planet. Information goods are practically free to copy and distribute.

Optimism about technological capabilities extends to decentralized visions of a better, more equal future. Mason and others are inspired by the open technology movement, arguing that digital technologies allow for community-based production and freely shared information assets. By making economic production possible in voluntary communities (Benkler 2006), rather than in markets or commercial hierarchies, open technology could, if supported and encouraged by government policy, lead to a more equitable society.

The institutional context school believes the solution is to rewrite the economic rules, and to raise awareness about inequality issues in ways that will create political pressure for change. The true opportunity for technology may reside in its use as a tool to encourage these necessary changes, for example by helping people educate themselves, and helping citizens organize for social change. For inequality researchers such as Piketty, the key to reducing inequality is to change policies, particularly taxation rules and governance structures that reduce tax on financial assets relative to taxes on more widely held real assets. More equitable taxation would require more transparency about asset ownership around the world, a challenge in today's transnational regulatory environment, but one where digital technology might be helpful. Cooperation across nations would be required to enforce tax laws, and reform intellectual property law. Technology could play many roles in this effort, increasing asset visibility or enforcing taxation law, but the emphasis on institutional context does not prioritize technology in the inequality story, either as a problem or a solution.

The task of restoring technology to its rightful place as an opportunity generator is not an easy one. There are multiple issues to address, and many different means to do so, in complex and non-transparent multinational environments. But are these remedies the only options? Is more digital-friendly education that upgrades analytic or STEM skills the best, or even the only, response to the new digitally mediated world we find ourselves in? Rewriting tax codes and building political awareness may be noble and worthwhile pursuits, but are there any other practices that might connect more directly to the daily reality of digital technology, and how technology creates and distributes wealth?

Our task will be to assess these different options for addressing the technology and inequality relationship, and perhaps generate new ones. In times of change, there are opportunities to test out new ideas. Traditional political coalitions are realigning. Digital technology is lowering the cost of many forms of experimentation and cooperation. What is lacking is a clear and compelling vision of what to do about inequality, and technology's role in it. What is the pathway for bringing opportunity back for future generations, particularly in the developed world? We will begin our search for new answers by looking at how wealth has shifted over the past 40 years in the most highly digital economies.

Notes

1. Visions of the PC-centric future ranged from emancipatory (Nelson 1987) to better functioning versions of existing economy and society (Gates et al. 1995).
2. Some of the most enthusiastic visions of the 'new economy' include Kelly (1999) and Tapscott (1996).
3. See World Economic Forum (2017) and Oxfam (2016).
4. For example, see Piketty and Saez (2003) and Atkinson et al. (2011).
5. As argued in Piketty's surprise bestseller (Piketty 2014).

6. Multiple resources available at United States Census Bureau (2016).
7. Best represented by the debate around *The Spirit Level* (Wilkinson and Pickett 2010).
8. The literature review in Lee (2015) has resources on gender and ethnic disparities in computer science education.
9. See Goldin and Katz (2009) for a summary of this literature.

REFERENCES

Atkinson, A. B., Piketty, T., & Saez, E. (2011). Top incomes in the long run of history. *Journal of Economic Literature, 49*(1), 3–71.

Bakos, Y. (1998). The emerging role of electronic marketplaces on the internet. *Communications of the ACM, 41*(8), 35–42.

Benkler, Y. (2006). *The wealth of networks: How social production transforms markets and freedom.* New Haven, CT: Yale University Press.

Brynjolfsson, E., & McAfee, A. (2014). *The second machine age: Work, progress, and prosperity in a time of brilliant technologies.* New York: WW Norton & Company.

Brynjolfsson, E., Hu, Y., & Smith, M. D. (2010). Research commentary—Long tails vs. superstars: The effect of information technology on product variety and sales concentration patterns. *Information Systems Research, 21*(4), 736–747.

Card, D., Lemieux, T., & Riddell, W. C. (2004). Unions and wage inequality. *Journal of Labor Research, 25*(4), 519–559.

Cingano, F. (2014). *Trends in income inequality and its impact on economic growth (1815–199X).* Retrieved from http://dx.doi.org/10.1787/5jxrjncwxv6j-en.

Citizens for Tax Justice. (2016). Fortune 500 companies hold a record $2.4 trillion offshore. Retrieved January 19, 2017, from http://ctj.org/ctjreports/2016/03/fortune_500_companies_hold_a_record_24_trillion_offshore.php.

Economic Policy Institute. (2017). Productivity and real median family income growth, 1947–2013|State of Working America. Retrieved February 23, 2017, from http://stateofworkingamerica.org/charts/productivity-and-real-median-family-income-growth-1947-2009/.

Elliott, M. S., & Kraemer, K. L. (Eds.). (2008). *Computerization movements and technology diffusion: From mainframes to ubiquitous computing.* Medford: Information Today Inc.

European Commission. (2016). State aid: Ireland gave illegal tax benefits to Apple worth up to €13 billion. Retrieved January 19, 2017, from http://europa.eu/rapid/press-release_IP-16-2923_en.htm.

Gates, B., Myhrvold, N., & Rinearson, P. (1995). *The road ahead.* New York: Viking Penguin.

Goldin, C. D., & Katz, L. F. (2009). *The race between education and technology.* Cambridge, MA: Harvard University Press.

Hilbert, M. (2014). Technological information inequality as an incessantly moving target: The redistribution of information and communication capacities between 1986 and 2010. *Journal of the Association for Information Science and Technology, 65*(4), 821–835.

Huddleston, C. (2016). 69% of Americans have less than $1,000 in savings. Retrieved January 18, 2017, from https://www.gobankingrates.com/personal-finance/data-americans-savings/.

Jones, C., & Klenow, P. (2016). Beyond GDP? Welfare across countries and time. *American Economic Review, 106*(9), 2426–2457.

Kelly, K. (1999). *New rules for the new economy: 10 radical strategies for a connected world.* New York: Penguin.

Kling, R. (Ed.). (1996). *Computerization and controversy: Value conflicts and social choices* (2nd ed.). San Diego, CA: Academic Press.

Kochhar, R., & Fry, R. (2014). Wealth inequality has widened along racial, ethnic lines since end of great recession. Retrieved January 18, 2017, from http://www.pewresearch.org/fact-tank/2014/12/12/racial-wealth-gaps-great-recession/.

Lee, A. (2015). Determining the effects of computer science education at the secondary level on STEM major choices in postsecondary institutions in the United States. *Computers & Education, 88,* 241–255.

Levy, S. (2001). *Hackers: Heroes of the computer revolution.* New York: Penguin.

Markoff, J. (2005). *What the Dormouse said: How the sixties counterculture shaped the personal computer industry.* New York: Penguin.

Mason, P. (2016). *Postcapitalism: A guide to our future.* New York: Farrar, Straus and Giroux.

Moody's Investor Service. (2016). US corporate cash pile, led by tech sector, to grow to $1.77 trillion by end of 2016. Retrieved January 23, 2017, from https://www.moodys.com/research/Moodys-US-corporate-cash-pile-led-by-tech-sector-to-PR_357576.

National Venture Capital Association. (2016). New survey reflects lack of women and minorities in senior investment roles at venture capital firms. Retrieved January 17, 2017, from http://nvca.org/pressreleases/new-survey-reflects-lack-women-minorities-senior-investment-roles-venture-capital-firms/.

Nelson, T. H. (1987). *Computer lib: Dream machines.* Redmond, WA: Tempus Books of Microsoft Press.

Oxfam. (2016). An economy for the 1%: How privilege and power in the economy drive extreme inequality and how this can be stopped. Retrieved January 15, 2017, from http://oxf.am/Znhx.

Piketty, T. (2014). *Capital in the twenty-first century* (A. Goldhammer, Trans.). Cambridge, MA: Harvard University Press.

Piketty, T., & Saez, E. (2003). Income inequality in the United States, 1913–1998. *Quarterly Journal of Economics, 118*(1), 1–39.

Ravallion, M. (2014). Income inequality in the developing world. *Science, 344*(6186), 851–855.

Reich, R. (1991). *The work of nations: Preparing ourselves for twenty-first century capitalism*. New York: Alfred Knopf.

Reich, R. (2016). *Saving capitalism: For the many, not the few*. New York: Vintage.

Rodriguez, S. (2016). It's time for silicon valley to stop making excuses on diversity. Retrieved January 16, 2017, from http://www.inc.com/salvador-rodriguez/silicon-valley-diversity-stop-excuses.html.

Sax, L. J., Lehman, K. J., Jacobs, J. A., Kanny, M. A., Lim, G., Monje-Paulson, L., et al. (2016). Anatomy of an enduring gender gap: The evolution of women's participation in computer science. *The Journal of Higher Education, 88*(2), 258–293.

Scott Morton, M. S. (Ed.). (1991). *The Corporation of the 1990s: Information technology and organizational transformation*. New York: Oxford University Press.

Sen, A. (1999). *Development as freedom*. New York: Oxford University Press.

Smith, M. R., & Marx, L. (1994). *Does technology drive history? The dilemma of technological determinism*. Cambridge, MA: MIT Press.

Sprague, S. (2014). What can labor productivity tell us about the U.S. economy? Retrieved January 15, 2017, from https://www.bls.gov/opub/btn/volume-3/what-can-labor-productivity-tell-us-about-the-us-economy.htm.

Stiglitz, J. E. (2012). *The price of inequality: How today's divided society endangers our future*. New York: WW Norton & Company.

Tapscott, D. (1996). *The digital economy: Promise and peril in the age of networked intelligence*. New York: McGraw-Hill.

United States Census Bureau. (2016). Income inequality. Retrieved January 15, 2017, from http://www.census.gov/topics/income-poverty/income-inequality.html.

USA Today. (2016). Diversity in silicon valley. Retrieved January 16, 2017, from http://www.usatoday.com/topic/3c5221f2-8f5a-414d-8f29-1ed23ac766a3/inequity-in-silicon-valley/.

Van Gelder, S. (2011). *This changes everything: Occupy Wall Street and the 99% movement*. San Francisco, CA: Berrett-Koehler Publishers.

Weinberg, G. M. (1998). *The psychology of computer programming* (Silver Anniversary Edition ed.). New York: Van Nostrand Reinhold.

Wilkinson, R., & Pickett, K. (2010). *The spirit level: Why greater equality makes societies stronger*. New York: Bloomsbury Press.

World Economic Forum. (2017). The global risks report (12th ed.). Retrieved January 15, 2017, from https://www.weforum.org/reports/the-global-risks-report-2017.

World Wealth & Income Database. (2017). WID. Retrieved February 23, 2017, from http://wid.world/data/.

CHAPTER 2

Information Technology and Wealth Concentration

Abstract This chapter describes shifts in private wealth in the United States since 1980, away from real assets toward financial assets, and away from the energy and commodity sectors of the economy toward information technology and finance. We describe how major digital technology companies, despite their variety, share basic similarities in terms of financial characteristics, such as profits, ownership, and a variety of business models. This chapter also explores how the scalability of digital technology affects the concentration of wealth.

Keywords Wealth concentration · Changes in wealth · Information technology sector · Financial assets · Scalability

2.1 The Great Wealth Shift

With rising income inequality since 1980 came an equally dramatic, if less discussed, shift in the nature of wealth. Piketty includes in his theory both wealth and income inequality, characterizing the relationship between wealth and income as wealth representing the 'weight of the past,' or previous accumulations of income, and income representing the present day. Wealth inequality is even higher than income inequality, as measured by Gini coefficients (Keister 2000). Piketty divides wealth into two types: financial assets, such as cash, bonds, and stock ownership, and real assets, such as housing and vehicles. The two types of financial assets differ in their ownership transparency, and how they are usually taxed. The owners of real properties are often easier to identify, and real property tends to be taxed on the full value of the asset every year while financial assets are often taxed only on the gains when an asset is sold.

The US economy since 1980 has been experiencing growing financialization, with a larger percent of the economy and its profits coming from financial activities rather than trade or production. Financialization can be seen in the growing percentage of corporate profits captured by the financial sector, and by the growing percentage of income coming from financial sources in households and non-financial companies (Krippner 2005).

Financialization has brought a shift in US household wealth from real to financial assets. Figure 2.1 summarizes the shifts in US household wealth. According to data from the US Census Bureau, financial assets

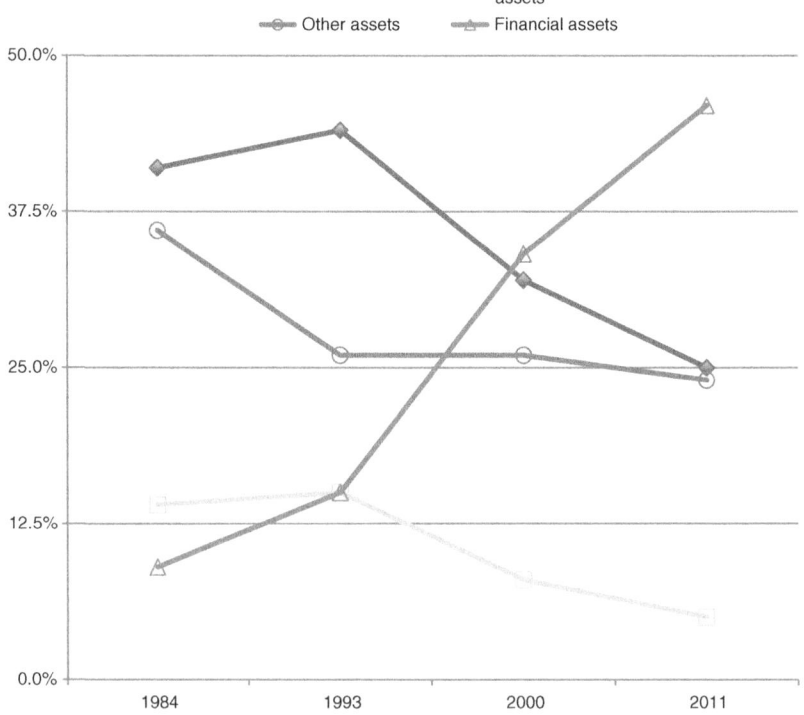

Fig. 2.1 *IEA* savings, money market, CD, interest checking; *other assets* vehicles, rental properties, business, unsecured liabilities, other. *Source* SIPP, US Census

have risen from 25 to over 50% of median household wealth between 1984 and 2011. Even with the decline of interest-bearing bank accounts, there has been explosive growth in household ownership of stocks, particularly in tax-advantaged retirement accounts. Real estate fell from 40 to 25% of median household wealth in the US during that same period, while the percentage of wealth in other hard assets, such as cars and furniture, has also declined.

The shift from real to financial wealth has underappreciated consequences for economic inequality. Real estate assets, though unequally distributed, are more equally distributed than financial assets, which tend to concentrate in high net worth households. By the 1990s, the top 10% of the wealthiest US households held 88.4% of stocks and mutual fund wealth and 91.8% of financial securities wealth, but only 31.7% of principal residence ownership wealth (Wolff 1998). The bottom half of all US households hold no financial assets at all beyond a small savings account. It is more difficult for the wealthy to escape taxes on real property, and there is greater transparency about asset ownership.

Financial asset ownership in US households is highly concentrated, whether held in private retirement accounts or private business ownership. As corporate profits have increased since 1980 as a percentage of GDP from about 5 to 10% of the US economy (U.S. Bureau of Economic Analysis 2017), a greater percentage of national income has shifted to the wealthiest households through capital gains, dividends, and share buybacks. Over this same period, corporate leaders have increased their emphasis on distributing wealth to shareholders rather than other business stakeholders, such as labor, local communities, or the environment (Jones and Felps 2013).

Changes in financial wealth ownership also interact with ethnic and gender inequality. During the 2007–2008 financial crisis, ethnic minority households in the US were disproportionately affected by the collapse in real estate values (Kochhar and Fry 2014), further concentrating wealth along ethnic lines. The wealth of single earner, female-led households was also disproportionately affected by the crisis.

The growth of financialization, and the shift in wealth toward financial assets, has been controversial. A recent presidential address of the American Finance Association asked whether the growth of the financial sector has been as positive for society as it has been for wealthy investors (Zingales 2015). Critics such as Stiglitz, Mason, and others wonder whether the finance sector is taking over the 'real' economy, encouraging volatility in asset values that the wealthiest can use to their advantage, buying distressed assets at 'fire sale' prices during times of crisis.

Within the shift from real to financial assets, there has been a second important wealth shift since 1980 in the ownership of large corporations, the value of which reflects the growth in profitability and reach of some sectors of the economy relative to others. These wealth shifts represent trillions of US dollars, enough to account for significant changes in wealth distribution.

The wealth contained in the equity ownership of the largest US publicly-traded companies can be divided into ten broad sectors, according to the GICS classification of companies.[1] If we group these sectors into three larger groupings, as shown in Fig. 2.2, a pattern becomes clearer. According to Siegel, the two industry sectors that have grown the most

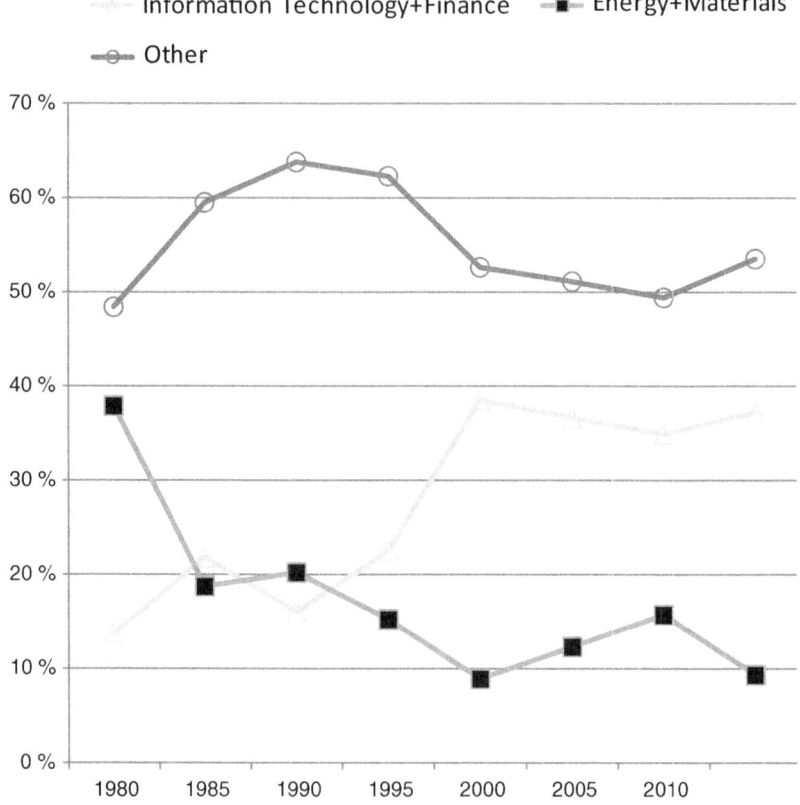

Fig. 2.2 Market capitalization of S&P 500 by sector type, United States, 1980–2015 (Standard and Poor's 2017)

since the 1980s in terms of financial value are information technology and finance, while the two sectors that have shrunk the most are energy and commodities (Siegel 2005). The two sectors involved in basic physical resources have declined significantly, from around 40 to 10% of market capitalization. The two fastest growing industry sectors, information technology and finance, have grown in proportion by roughly the same amount, the value of the virtualized economy just about swapping places with the value of primary physical production. The remaining other six sectors, if we lump them together as the traditional or 'real' economy, have maintained a fairly consistent value at 50–60% of market capitalization.

In addition to equities, other kinds of financial assets reflect this wealth shift. Corporations around the world have been building large cash and investment stockpiles rather than investing in their own operations or distributing wealth to other corporate stakeholders beyond share owners. As noted above, almost half the total corporate cash stockpile overseas is held by information technology companies.

One way of interpreting this wealth shift would be as a transformation from a more material to a more virtual economy. At the most abstract level, the purpose of both the financial and the information technology sectors is to provide information and services that lead to better decision-making, and resource allocation, in the 'real' economy. Rather than limiting themselves to the role of assistants, though, both the information technology and finance sectors are themselves becoming an increasing share of the economy through their virtualized products and services. Both of these sectors have become the most effective in generating profits and creating financial wealth.

These shifts in wealth since 1980 provide a new lens for exploring the relationship between technology and inequality. What is it about the information technology sector that makes it such a wealth-generating machine? And does this shift in wealth to the information technology sector have a different impact on inequality than wealth concentrated in other sectors of the economy? If there is a wealth concentration effect because of the information technology sector, is it due to some inherent characteristic of technology, as the technological school would lead us to believe? Or is there something distinctive about the way the information technology sector has taken advantage of the institutional context? These wealth shifts could be more about the writing of intellectual property rules in favor of technology companies, or about the favorable taxation treatment they receive, or perhaps because of some previously unexamined combination of the two.

2.2 Virtualized Economy: How the Information Technology Sector Is Different Financially

With wealth shifting toward the information technology sector, it becomes important to examine the business practices of large technology corporations. Specific business practices provide a conceptual link between technological capabilities and features of the broader economic environment. Though a technological deterministic argument claims that technology affects the world directly, digital technology is realized through specific business and industry practices.

How are technology sector companies different? Rising equity values, combined with some of the largest cash stockpiles, are both evidence of the unusually strong profitability of large technology companies over time, taken as a group. Both of these wealth stockpiles, equity and cash, confer significant power upon these corporations. They provide the currency to acquire other companies, to hire the most expensive engineers and managers, and to attract the interest of investors in secondary financial markets, such as the stock market. Some of these acquisitions offer extreme examples of wealth being concentrated into the hands of very few investors and employees, such as the multi-billion dollar acquisitions of very small startups, like Instagram and WhatsApp by Facebook. In each case, hundreds of millions of dollars went to a small team of investors, founders, and early employees.

Many of the channels for distributing the wealth captured by large technology companies appear to be highly concentrated. The ownership and management of the high-growth technology firms being acquired by this wealth is concentrated in the richer parts of society, with compensation disproportionately placed in the hands of a small group of managers and engineers. The wealth distributed to shareholders, through rising dividends and share buybacks, also finds its way primarily into the hands of wealthy households. Share buybacks in particular have increased in size to the point where they account for almost all the profits of large US corporations (Wang and Bost 2014), including technology firms. Apple alone has authorized over $150 billion in share buybacks, spending $10 billion on share repurchases in a recent quarter when their total operating cash flow was $11.6 billion (Apple Insider 2016). Clearly, the channeling of wealth to the already wealthy has an impact on inequality.

Low levels of taxation are common for large technology firms. For the institutional context school, taxation policy is one of the key drivers of economic inequality. The real rate of taxation for large technology companies is often lower than other large companies (Kim 2015). As we have seen above, large technology companies can use international subsidiaries to pay less tax on parts of their income than their real economy counterparts. As might be expected, the fraction of assets that are intangible, particularly intellectual property, is high in large technology companies. And intellectual property assets are more effectively used as part of an international tax avoidance scheme than other kinds of wealth (Griffith et al. 2014).

For public technology companies, total compensation or wages might be relatively smaller due to the higher revenue and profits generated per worker, but there is little research to confirm this. Wages in general are high in technology firms, and overall technology sector employment growth continues to grow (Hathaway and Kallerman 2012). Large technology companies use stock options and shares as a larger proportion of compensation than other similar companies (Anderson et al. 2000), which is likely to be unevenly distributed even within the companies themselves. Though beliefs in the power of a key founder or CEO are just as prevalent in the technology sector, there is little evidence that executive compensation is higher in technology companies relative to their size. The largest technology companies are able to generate a large amount of revenue with relatively few employees. For example, employees at Apple, Facebook, and Google each generated more than $1 million of revenue per capita in 2015 (Rosoff 2016).

Technology sector companies consistently have some of the largest profit margins, and absolute profits, of all industry sectors (Chen 2015). Large profits and margins might come from a relative lack of competition, in the most extreme case because of a monopoly position. Are technology companies more likely to be monopolies? Large technology companies, such as Microsoft, Google, and Apple, have faced anti-trust lawsuits and enforcement attempts from governments for decades, but few of those attempts have resulted in an order to break up a monopoly. Despite the lack of anti-trust actions taken by governments, except for fines that represent small fractions of their profits, effective monopoly or duopoly is a feature of many parts of the digital economy, including search engines, social media, personal computer operating systems, and mobile device operating systems. Even newer markets such as sharing economy hiring sites, and online retail sites such as Amazon, appear to be headed toward further market concentration. The network effects of digital technology may naturally encourage monopolistic wealth concentration.

Not all digital technology companies are large enough to be in the S&P 500. There are at least two different types of small and medium-sized enterprises (SMEs) that are technology startups. One type is technology intensive, high growth, and backed by high-risk investors such as 'angels,' or venture capital. Another group of startups is more 'mom and pop,' consisting of small independent contractors with few or no employees, for example a local sales and support business. For technology-intensive, venture-backed companies, there appears to be a wealth concentration effect in which members of a small founding team each stand to make multi-millions, or even billions, with the right acquisition or public share offering. The number of key employees with stock options is relatively small. Much of this wealth will flow to a small group of people. Investors in high-growth technology companies tend to be wealthier, and in some countries are required to have a minimum net worth in the millions of dollars before they can invest. With institutional investors comes the promise of a more equitable sharing of wealth created by the technology sector, but financial asset ownership is still fairly highly concentrated in the broader economy.

For the smaller, slow-or no-growth SMEs, there is a lack of data on their wealth concentration effects. While studies suggests the birth rate of high-growth technology startups is declining (Haltiwanger et al. 2014), and overall startup formation is declining in advanced economies such as the US (Haltiwanger et al. 2015), we know little about new business formation for this more common type of SME. We also don't have much evidence about the effect the technology sector has on wealth concentration in other industry sectors, beyond a general recognition that digital technology investment is broadly associated with increases in investment return (Mithas et al. 2012). The best hope for inequality reduction through the technology sector might be by encouraging opportunity in other sectors. Perhaps the rise of online shopping allows small retail businesses to play on an equal playing field relative to large retailers, or local micro-entrepreneurs could effectively compete in the hotel industry with multinational chains through platforms such as Airbnb.

2.3 Value Creation and Value Capture in the Information Technology Sector

The distinction between value creation and value capture has been essential in entrepreneurial and strategic thinking (Teece 2010). Value creation is the set of activities that transform a combination of resources and capabilities into a product or service that has a value higher than the total cost of production, whereas value capture is the ability to realize that profit through specific activities performed by the customer. Inventors may create something wonderful and new, which is the value creation piece of the puzzle. But history is filled with examples of inventors not benefitting financially from their successful inventions, which is the value capture side. Sometimes this is a deliberate choice, as in the case of the World Wide Web, which was freely shared with the world. At other times, the inability to profit from one's own inventions is due to luck, subterfuge, or being outmaneuvered, with cases such as IBM or Xerox PARC versus Microsoft or Apple from the Personal Computing era often mentioned as prime examples.

In many ways, value creation and capture can be seen as the core problem of entrepreneurship and strategy. New value creation depends on invention, but value capture requires something more. From a wealth-generating perspective, there must be a realistic mechanism through which value creators can benefit from their labors.

The value creation capabilities of information technology are many and varied, and have been growing over time as measured by pure technical performance. Digital technology hardware has been improving at an exponential rate for decades, as predicted by Moore's law in the 1970s (Mack 2015), and the progress surprisingly continues. Digital storage and networking power also continue to increase, opening new possibilities for creating valuable products and services. Digital technology has improved to such an extent that Christensen argues technological capability has surpassed what companies and consumers can use effectively, a phenomenon he calls 'performance overshoot.'[2] Laptops and mobile phones can execute billions of instructions per second, much more power than most people need for their everyday uses, such as writing a text message or looking at a web page.

However, this surplus of raw digital power seems to be finding new uses. New artificial intelligence applications, rather than relying on elegant theories and sophisticated understandings of how the world works, are instead relying on brute force power and huge data sets to come up with answers. Speech recognition, vision processing, big data analysis, and autonomous vehicles are just some of the most current examples of digital technology's potential to create new value through massive processing power and large data sets.

Beyond the underlying hardware of digital processing, storage, and networking, we also have the value creating capability of software. Modern software provides a vast set of building blocks for others to build upon, as giant code bases such as the Linux kernel combine and condense millions of programmer hours of effort into a resource that others can freely use and build upon. The rich universe of application software continues to grow in power and usefulness.

For Teece and others, value capture can happen in different ways. The most straightforward method is to sell a product or service. But when a particular product or service is easy to copy or use for free, direct sales may not be the most effective option, as many an entrepreneur has discovered when their new invention was copied and sold by other parties. One of the most fundamental forms of value capture in these circumstances is intellectual property protection Copyright and patent licensing are commonly used value capture models in the technology sector that have advantages over trying to directly sell a product.

Another popular method of value capture is through complementary assets, or by selling products and services that combine with something else made available at low cost, or for free. For digital technology, it is sometimes easier to sell the hardware rather than the software, or to sell a networking service rather than the content available on that service, where one part of a combination can be subsidized or given away for free while other parts are sold.

The value captured can then be shared across the different parties that collaborate to create value. For example, an app store could share a percentage of sales with the software authors, and keep a percentage for themselves. Value can be created by other groups, even the users themselves. An online fan site could make a product more attractive and valuable, or an online discussion group could answer support questions. The value created by users could be shared with them directly, for example by giving resources to user groups and clubs, or the value could be kept inside the company, for example if user discussion groups are used as a substitute for paid product support.

In addition to value creation and capture, the other key concept connecting technology and wealth is the concept of a business model. The business model is a conceptual understanding, or a hypothesis, of how value creation and capture happen (Teece 2010). The business model is implemented, and then tested against reality. Business models that do not fare well can, at least in theory, be experimented with and improved.

What is new with digital technology is the sheer variety of possible business models, along with more powerful ways of testing the viability of those models. As a famous example, consider the Google search engine. Through their unique algorithm that uses web page links as votes for the quality of web pages, Google was able to create value: a search engine that returned better, more relevant results than anything that came before it. But what should the business model of search technology be? Sell web searches as a subscription service? Sell advertisements that appear next to search results? Sell preferred results in a web search, allowing paid results to be shown first? Or sell consumer information about searches to third parties? Or some combination of all of these?

Other search companies eventually copied the techniques that led to superior search results, but none were able to match Google's successful business model, which successfully combined a number of elements. First, their search engine returned two sets of results, the most relevant 'organic' results, and a set of paid results offered by advertisers. Keeping these two sets of results separated increased the credibility of results, and even the paid results maintained a level of quality by using a unique selection method. The advertisements that generated the most revenue through user clicks, and thus were perceived as useful, were displayed at the top of the paid results rather than advertisers who had paid the most. This model led to more clicks, better results, and maximum revenue for Google. Combined with a self-service advertisement creation and bidding technology, the Google search engine model continues to be wildly profitable. The vast majority of revenue for Google's parent company, Alphabet, continues to be paid search advertising. Google has added to the business model a sophisticated advertising network, which skillfully matches its inventory of advertisements to another large inventory of online publishers.

After a long development period without any revenue streams, Facebook also settled upon self-service advertising as their main business model. Their business model includes conventional advertising, and, additionally, an ability to promote status updates and other content through social networks. The model has become extremely profitable, with businesses now in the position of having to pay Facebook in order to communicate with their own followers. The Twitter platform has also experimented with sponsored content as a business model, but with less dramatic financial success.

Apple and Microsoft, in contrast, stick mostly to the business model of sales. Apple sells its digital hardware at profit margins upwards of 50%, while mostly giving the complementary asset of software away for free. The hardware sales would be nowhere near as profitable, however, without the seamless user experience that brings Apple hardware and software together in an easy-to-use combination. Though mostly using sales, Apple does experiment with other business models for different product lines, such as subscriptions for online 'cloud' storage services, and some of their business models change over time, such as digital music which is moving from sales to a subscription model.

The Microsoft model is predominantly to sell systems and application software, relying on other companies to produce the complementary hardware to run the software effectively and cheaply. Where as software companies might have difficulty competing with free, unauthorized copies of their own products, digital software providers can switch to a business model of charging for complementary services, and even tolerate certain levels of privacy in limited markets to generate demand and market share.

Still other digital technology companies pursue a transaction model, which charges a percentage fee every time buyers and sellers are matched. In the new sharing economy, Uber and Airbnb use this model to match consumers and service providers, taking a substantial cut of every transaction. In these cases, companies charge up to 20–30% simply for being the matchmaker, and can modify the percentage in real time depending on market conditions. Large technology companies, too, are eager to pursue a mix of business models. Apple charges up to 30% for purchases in their app store, which cost very little to deliver.

Technology companies constantly experiment with different business models to find the best financial results. The career-oriented social network LinkedIn has multiple revenue streams, charging for job advertisements, sending messages within their network, and for premium services to hiring companies. Other digital companies such as Netflix have found new models for existing businesses, in this case using a subscription model for movies instead of purchases or ticket sales. Overall, it appears technology companies are able to experiment, and potentially succeed, with new business models in more traditional industries that have faced financial challenges, and that digital technology companies have the freedom, capability, and creativity to find new business models. This flexibility has allowed technology companies to become masters of value capture in ways other institutions have traditionally found difficult to compete against. There is constant experimentation, both in terms of the business model technology companies choose, and also in terms of the variables used. How much commission should they charge? What should subscription fees be for different types of subscribers? How much should be charged to expose users to different kinds of content? Digital technology companies have the data, and the ability, to experiment with their offerings. Companies such as Netflix are running thousands of experiments per day on their own customers trying to optimize business results (Urban et al. 2016), with such precision that even the image to click on for watching a movie is constantly being experimented with. At what point does a mastery of value capture become a mechanism for concentrating wealth?

2.4 The Scalability of Information Technology and Wealth Concentration

Scalability is the ability to grow in size or scope quickly and at low cost. Scalability is one of the most pronounced features of digital technology, thanks to the Internet technology infrastructure that has penetrated many parts of the globe. Eighty percent of the developed world has Internet access, with 50% of the entire world projected to have access by 2020 (International Telecommunication Union 2016). Internet-enabled mobile phones have swept the globe, leading to greater than 100% penetration rates in parts of the developed world.

With a global technology infrastructure, digital technology becomes easy to scale. Digital infrastructure is physical, but it is also based on common standards, protocols, and software. When operating system software becomes widely shared, programmers gain the ability to execute code on millions, or billions, of devices around the world, and because operating system software tends to form monopolies or duopolies, application software is that much easier to scale.

The Internet provides the most powerful example in human history of a common standards base providing the infrastructure needed for scalability. With the common set of services built around the open TCP/IP protocol, the Internet provides a generic, low-cost data communication and transportation system. With some notable exceptions, the Internet provides a level playing field for these services, not giving communication traffic priority to large companies and institutions over small companies and individuals. With a working connection and a valid IP address, the global Internet does all the work of moving data around the world, whether one is a giant corporation or a hobbyist in a garage. This is a huge burden lifted from anyone who wants to write software, or offer a digital service, that can serve millions or billions of people. The most notable exceptions to this level playing field are the state actors who control and monitor an increasing fraction of Internet traffic.

The scalability of digital technology has manifested itself in the low-cost cloud computing movement. Students or startups can launch their code in the cloud at an extremely low initial cost, using the same advanced technology infrastructure available to the largest corporations. As the number of customers increases, the costs and complexity serving them increase only gradually (Armbrust et al. 2010).

The scalability of the digital world is also related to the modularity of information technology. Software design offers the possibility of breaking problems or products into smaller parts then recombining them. When software is made openly available, it becomes easier to build on top of the work of others rather than forcing programmers to recreate every solution on their own. Software modularity makes it possible for thousands of volunteer programmers to coordinate themselves, each working on their own piece of the problem and combining them later. With software scalability, small groups of programmers can create sophisticated products quickly and achieve a global scale. When Instagram was acquired by Facebook in 2012, 13 employees had created a service in less than 2 years that served 30 million users (Luckerson 2016). The Internet, software tools, and the availability of app stores made this level of scalability possible.

We know the scalability of the digital world relates to wealth inequality in at least two ways. First, it brings to life the superstar dynamic in which a few superstars can offer the best mobile app, the best song, or the best video on a massive scale. If consumers are only willing to choose the absolute best, then, theoretically, this should lead to wealth concentration for a few top performers or creators. The superstar effect, however, appears to be somewhat uneven so far. There are segments of the book and music industry where only the biggest stars sell products and make a living from their content directly, whereas in other areas, such as university lecturers, the superstar effect has yet to take hold. The theory of where and when digital superstar effects arise in digital content and software still requires further investigation.

A second mechanism for scalability leading to wealth concentration is through automation. The knowledge or skill needed to perform a task can be captured once, encoded into software instructions, then copied and delivered at extremely low cost. Technology has extended the scope of automation in ways beyond what we recently imagined possible, such as with autonomous vehicles and voice recognition. Frey and Osborne (2017) famously calculated that almost half of all jobs were at risk of being automated in the near future.

The best evidence for automation comes from the professions that have already been severely reduced in size, such as travel agents or paid journalists. Compared to the number of new jobs created in technology-related fields, the fear is that new jobs will not be plentiful enough, or will require expensive skills or rare aptitudes to fill. The limits of automation can still be found in jobs where the knowledge required is not explicit enough, or involves some level of physical skill. However, speculation about AI and robots in the future, even the near future, cannot account for the last 40 years of increasing wealth inequality.

The relationship between digital technology and wealth concentration is more clearly seen in the business practices of the technology sector and the resulting wealth shifts than in the more abstract arguments about automation and superstar effects. Regardless, there are many pathways to wealth concentration in our new digital world. In the next chapter, we take a closer look at the business models replacing markets with digital platforms, a model at the center of many of the largest technology companies.

Notes

1. The GCIS classification added a new 11th sector, Real Estate, in 2016. This sector was previously a part of the Finance sector. We use the older 10 sector classification for historical consistency.
2. What Christensen called a 'performance overshoot' (Christensen 2013).

References

Anderson, M. C., Banker, R. D., & Ravindran, S. (2000). Executive compensation in the information technology industry. *Management Science, 46*(4), 530–547.

Apple Insider. (2016). Apple adds $50B to capital return program, increases quarterly dividend by 10%. Retrieved January 20, 2017, from http://appleinsider.com/articles/16/04/26/apple-adds-50b-to-capital-return-program-announces-10-dividend-increase-.

Armbrust, M., Fox, A., Griffith, R., Joseph, A. D., Katz, R., Konwinski, A., ... Stoica, I. (2010). A view of cloud computing. *Communications of the ACM, 53*(4), 50–58.

Chen, L. (2015). The most profitable industries in 2016. Retrieved January 20, 2017, from http://www.forbes.com/sites/liyanchen/2015/12/21/the-most-profitable-industries-in-2016/.

Christensen, C. (2013). *The innovator's dilemma: When new technologies cause great firms to fail*. Cambridge, MA: Harvard Business Review Press.

Frey, C. B., & Osborne, M. A. (2017). The future of employment: How susceptible are jobs to computerisation? *Technological Forecasting and Social Change, 114*, 254–280.

Griffith, R., Miller, H., & O'Connell, M. (2014). Ownership of intellectual property and corporate taxation. *Journal of Public Economics, 112*, 12–23.

Haltiwanger, J., Decker, R., & Jarmin, R. (2015). *Top ten signs of declining business dynamism and entrepreneurship in the US*. Paper presented at the Kauffman Foundation New Entrepreneurial Growth Conference, Kansas City, MO.

Haltiwanger, J., Hathaway, I., & Miranda, J. (2014). Declining business dynamism in the US high-technology sector. Retrieved January 20, 2017, from https://papers.ssrn.com/sol3/papers2.cfm?abstract_id=2397310.

Hathaway, I., & Kallerman, P. (2012, December). *Technology works: High-tech employment and wages in the United States*. San Francisco: Bay Area Economic Institute.

International Telecommunication Union. (2016). ITU ICT facts and figures 2016. Retrieved January 20, 2017, from http://www.itu.int/en/ITU-D/Statistics/Documents/facts/ICTFactsFigures2016.pdf.

Jones, T. M., & Felps, W. (2013). Shareholder wealth maximization and social welfare: A utilitarian critique. *Business Ethics Quarterly, 23*(02), 207–238.

Keister, L. A. (2000). *Wealth in America: Trends in wealth inequality*. New York: Cambridge University Press.

Kim, E. (2015). Tech giants are paying a lot less tax than some of the biggest companies in the US. Retrieved January 20, 2017, from http://www.

businessinsider.com/tech-companies-have-lower-effective-tax-rates-than-others-2015-12.
Kochhar, R., & Fry, R. (2014). Wealth inequality has widened along racial, ethnic lines since end of great recession. Retrieved January 18, 2017, from http://www.pewresearch.org/fact-tank/2014/12/12/racial-wealth-gaps-great-recession/.
Krippner, G. R. (2005). The financialization of the American economy. *Socio-Economic Review, 3*(2), 173–208.
Luckerson, V. (2016). Here's proof that Instagram was one of the smartest acquisitions ever. Retrieved January 20, 2017, from http://time.com/4299297/instagram-facebook-revenue/.
Mack, C. (2015). The multiple lives of Moore's law. *IEEE Spectrum, 52*(4), 31.
Mithas, S., Tafti, A., Bardhan, I., & Goh, J. M. (2012). Information technology and firm profitability: Mechanisms and empirical evidence. *MIS Quarterly, 36*(1), 205–224.
Rosoff, M. (2016). Here's how much each employee at a big tech company like Apple or Facebook is worth. Retrieved January 20, 2017, from http://www.businessinsider.com/revenue-per-employee-at-apple-facebook-google-others-2016-2.
Siegel, J. J. (2005). *The future for investors: Why the tried and the true triumphs over the bold and the new*. New York: Crown Business.
Standard and Poor's. (2017). Historical S&P 500 sector weightings by decade. Retrieved February 23, 2017, from http://www.sectorspdr.com/sectorspdr/IDCO.Client.Spdrs.DocumentLibrary/SectorResearchUpload/GetPdfDocumentByFullName?category=All%20Funds%20Documents&subcategory=Document%20Resources&title=10%20Year%20Sector%20Returns.
Teece, D. J. (2010). Business models, business strategy and innovation. *Long Range Planning, 43*(2), 172–194.
U.S. Bureau of Economic Analysis. (2017). Corporate profits after tax (without IVA and CCAdj). Retrieved January 20, 2017, from https://fred.stlouisfed.org/series/CP.
Urban, S., Sreenivasan, R., & Kannan, V. (2016). It's all A/Bout testing: The Netflix experimentation platform. Retrieved January 20, 2017, from http://techblog.netflix.com/2016/04/its-all-about-testing-netflix.html.
Wang, L., & Bost, C. (2014). S&P 500 companies spend almost all profits on buybacks. Retrieved January 20, 2017, from https://www.bloomberg.com/news/articles/2014-10-06/s-p-500-companies-spend-almost-all-profits-on-buybacks-payouts.
Wolff, E. N. (1998). Recent trends in the size distribution of household wealth. *The Journal of Economic Perspectives, 12*(3), 131–150.
Zingales, L. (2015). Presidential address: Does finance benefit society? *The Journal of Finance, 70*(4), 1327–1363.

CHAPTER 3

The Digital Economy: New Markets, New Gatekeepers

Abstract This chapter reviews debates about the Internet and the new digital economy. A unique aspect of digital technology is its potential to transform not only every stage of production, distribution, and consumption, but also the very mechanisms used to coordinate and regulate the economy. A digitally mediated economy, where digital technology, data, and algorithms sit between buyers and sellers, is contrasted against more traditional 'perfect,' or 'free' market theory. The unique features of digitally mediated markets include network effects and winner-take-all dynamics, the drive to own exclusive data, and the use of secretive algorithms.

Keywords Perfect markets · Digital intermediaries · New economy Winner-take-all · Algorithms

3.1 The Theory of Free Markets and Perfect Information

To understand how the digital economy affects the way markets work, we need to start with a theory of how traditional markets work. Stiglitz and other have summarized the main features of perfectly competitive markets.[1] The most basic requirement of perfectly competitive markets is, of course, true competition. A small set of buyers or sellers should not be able to set their own prices. There should not be any

© The Author(s) 2017
J.P. Allen, *Technology and Inequality*,
DOI 10.1007/978-3-319-56958-1_3

barriers preventing new buyers and sellers from entering a market. Every buyer and seller must be easily found, or discoverable, by every market participant.

Imperfect competition can arise from a number of sources. Externalities are one form of imperfection. Negative externalities are costs imposed on those who are not party to a transaction or decision, such as when a manufacturer pollutes the air that other people breathe, whether they use the products made or not. Externalizing costs can give some producers an artificial advantage.

Another imperfection comes from incomplete markets. In complete markets, the risk of every possible negative outcome can be managed through the purchase of insurance, or other kinds of financial instruments, like options. If perfect risk markets are not available, those parties who are better able to tolerate risk will be at an advantage, usually the already wealthy and powerful.

Most relevant to our discussion of digital mediation is the idea that perfect markets require perfect information. All the information needed to evaluate the price and quality of every product, and every service, needs to be known by every potential buyer and seller. The condition where some parties have relevant price and quality information and others do not is known as 'information asymmetry' (Greenwald and Stiglitz 1986). Information asymmetries arise when sellers know more about the quality of a specific product than a typical buyer, as might be the case with a used-car sale. Another form of information asymmetry occurs when sellers have a higher quality product, but there is a cost for signaling that quality difference to buyers. For example, sellers might have to pay for advertising, which may or may not be effective, or obtain verification from a third party.

The rapidly increasing capabilities of digital technology fueled the belief that markets would become more perfect in a digital age, and information more plentiful. Buyers and sellers should see fewer barriers to buying or selling, and there should be more information about negative outcomes and risks, leading to better economic decisions. For the business strategist, however, escaping perfect competition, with its low or zero profitability, is a top priority (Kim and Mauborgne 2005). Each feature of a perfectly competitive market can be turned on its head, serving as a guide for how to create sustained competitive advantages that generate higher profits (Porter 2008).

Digital technology can be used to create competitive advantage and escape perfect competition. One way this can occur is by creating a unique resource or capability, placing a company in the role of a monopoly provider. Digital technology might also be used to create barriers to entry by controlling the channels through which consumers receive information about alternatives. But the most potentially powerful, and perhaps slightly ironic strategy in digitally mediated markets is to possess information others do not have.

Economists distinguish between activities that create wealth and activities that extract wealth from others by virtue of ownership.[2] Wealth extraction activities are called rent, or rent-seeking, originally referring to the rent charged by owners of real assets. The idea of rent-seeking has been extended to include monopoly profits, quotas, and all other departures from competitive markets that enrich individuals at the expense of the greater social welfare. For digital technology, the question becomes how much economic wealth comes from creating new value, and how much from rent-seeking.

Predictions of a new digital economy were common after the Internet became open to commercial activity in the 1990s.[3] Three main arguments were offered about the impact of digital technologies on markets. First, there was the operation of markets themselves. Second, there was the question of what kinds of economic players would benefit the most from digital markets. Third, there was the question of whether market transactions would be used more frequently versus companies doing things on their own.

In the 1990s, digital technology was predicted to lead to more perfect, more 'frictionless' markets.[4] Sources of friction include search costs, or the costs of finding a product or service, and information about their prices and quality (Bakos 1998). The Internet was seen as the perfect technology for reducing search costs because product and price information would be available to everyone on the Internet, anywhere in the world, practically instantaneously, and for almost zero cost. This was also true for the developing world, where rural farms and fisheries could obtain better price information for the first time through Internet-enabled kiosks and mobile phones.[5] The apparent validity of these predictions was reinforced by new Internet sites for highly visible consumer purchases, such as hotel rooms and airline tickets, giving millions of people direct experience with the benefits of reduced search costs and easier discoverability. As impressive as these advances have been, search cost reductions have varied. The world of travel booking remains complex, with fewer than 20% of hotel rooms being booked through online travel agencies. Not every digital intervention in the developing world to provide better pricing information to farmers has made an impact (Fafchamps and Minten 2012). Search costs remain subject to the strategic choices of buyers and sellers, who may or may not participate in specific technology platforms, and who have to make specific choices about how they develop and deploy new technology.

A second prediction about digital markets was that perfect information would level the competitive playing field, allowing smaller businesses and entrepreneurs to compete as equals against the largest corporations. Customers would be able to find new businesses, no matter what their size or market power, and transact with them directly. Some new digital technologies, such as restaurant review sites, have created more business for small, independent restaurants at the expense of larger restaurant chains (Luca 2016). However, most small businesses continue to lack the resources necessary to fully benefit from new digital technologies (Stockdale and Standing 2004). New digital intermediaries, including review sites, use a variety of methods to help buyers discover businesses, not all of which are equally friendly to small or new businesses.

A third prediction was that greater efficiency in electronic markets would encourage companies to purchase more from outside contractors, and do fewer things themselves. With digital technology reducing not only search costs, but also the costs of signing contracts and monitoring performance, the Internet was thought to favor a world of smaller, more nimble companies connecting via market transactions rather than a world with a few giant corporations. Early evidence pointed to size reduction in companies that use more digital technology (Brynjolfsson et al. 1994), but, in the US economy as a whole, the fraction of people employed by larger firms has slightly increased, not decreased, since 1980 (Fort et al. 2013). There has been growth in the use of non-market transactions outside of traditional company boundaries, such as in open source software projects and crowdsourcing communities, but the number of labor hours involved is still a tiny fraction of the overall economy.

Overall, we find a mixed picture of more perfect information and competition in digital markets. Some markets have experienced improvements, but significant information asymmetries remain in others, sometimes by deliberate design. Even in the case of financial markets, which theoretically should be the closest to providing perfect information, the story has been mixed. Some financial markets, such as retail stock markets, have increased their transparency and lowered their intermediation costs. But in other ways, such as high-frequency trading and the creation of exotic new financial instruments traded over the counter, financial markets are arguably less transparent than in previous decades. Stiglitz argues that the cost of financial intermediation for the most basic function of finance, making loans, has actually increased in recent decades. The argument that digital technology leads to more perfect markets depends on another crucial assumption: that those markets are mediated in an even-handed and transparent manner, an assumption we look at in the following section.

3.2 Mediated Versus Perfect Markets

As we have seen above, many of the arguments about digital markets assume no one group receives favorable treatment, and the organization running the market will not control transactions for their own benefit. Because the market is seen as a self-governing mechanism, classic theories of perfect markets tend not to focus on the operation of the market itself.

In the digital world, there are many ways a market can mediate a relationship between buyers and sellers. Consider online searches for product information. In the US, over 80% of consumers search online before buying a product (Morrison 2014). About half of those online investigations begin with a search engine. Search engines provide many different methods for deciding which results appear first, or at all, in a request for information. Search engines can decide how, and to what extent, payments by sellers affect the order of results. Having a top search result is critical from a market discovery point of view because few consumers ever look beyond the first page of search results. Another half of online product searches in the US begin with a single technology company, Amazon (Soper 2016). The Amazon digital marketplace makes many choices about which sellers appear at the top of search results, often including Amazon itself.

Digitally-mediated markets possess two new technical capabilities allowing them to depart from the ideal of perfect markets One is the algorithm, or computational method, used to produce results for any search request. For the Google search algorithm, results are determined through a method that automatically weighs and combines over 250 different factors, with some unknown degree of manual manipulation.

It is not only the complexity of the algorithm that makes digitally-mediated markets different; there is also the algorithm's ability to evolve, and its secretive nature. The details of the algorithm are not revealed to the public. The algorithm itself changes regularly in response to new technologies, the results of user experiments, and attempts by sellers to manipulate the algorithm and earn a lucrative top search result. In some cases, the digital mediation company itself may not be completely aware of how the algorithm will perform in every situation.

Online retail markets such as Amazon also use algorithms to determine the results of product searches. While Google has faced questions about whether it favors its own sites in search results (White and Bodoni 2016), possibly abusing its position as a digital mediator for its own gain, Amazon is additionally complicated by being a seller on its own platform. Amazon can choose to favor their own products in their search algorithm (or not) without restriction. Amazon can decide when and how to display additional information for product searches, such as online reviews, substitute products, or even competitors. All of these challenges can make the prospect of competing with the company that controls the marketplace more complex than one that executes transactions through a traditional perfect market (Schmid 2016).

Just because a market is digitally mediated does not mean sellers will be treated unequally, deliberately or not. Newer or smaller sellers might even be favored in the search results. But a digitally mediated market does imply that the matching of buyers and sellers is subject to the strategy, goals, and pressures faced by the organization that mediates the market. For-profit corporations face a variety of pressures, even companies as large and profitable as the digital technology giants. Google, for example, is sufficiently profitable that it can buffer itself from many of the pressures of financial markets, famously using a percentage of its revenues to invest in new projects that are not likely to make money in the near future. Special-share ownership structures, such as multiple classes of shares with differential voting rights, help technology companies such as Google's parent company, Alphabet, preserve independence in the face of shareholder demands to contain costs and increase profits. The significant cash holdings of Apple, Microsoft, and other technology giants allow them to fund large dividend and buyback programs, further keeping investor demands at bay. But even companies as powerful as

Alphabet face pressures to improve their business models and place more weight on the needs of key stakeholders in their business models. The advertisers and sellers upon which Alphabet depends will seek guarantees that search results attract customers in a cost-effective manner.

A second new technical capability of digital mediation is the possession of unique information. A digitally mediated market offers the mediator the advantage of access to a unique database of buyer and seller preferences. This unique data set can be used to more precisely target offers and advertising messages, which can be as simple as repeating back what a buyer has searched for in the past, but can grow in sophistication as market participants build more elaborate profiles through more searches and transactions. Short of government intervention, or deliberate decisions to share data, no other parties have access to this information. By combining this unique data with other supporting services, such as easy payment, digital technology offers to consumers an experience that feels like the 'frictionless' market promised by early visions of the Internet. Digital mediation through a single technology company raises the question of how the value created by this improved buying experience will be shared, or captured, by the mediator.

Digital mediation makes it possible to implement new kinds of business models that are less dependent on product sales. Encouraging buyers to pay for digital content can be challenging, given the ease of digital copying and the many free alternatives available online. In this case, taking a percentage of a transaction that connects buyer and seller through a digital platform is sometimes an easier task. As long as a digital mediator keeps buyers and sellers connecting through their platform, value is captured and profits are made. Because there are many areas of the economy where potential buyers and sellers cannot easily reach either other, because of search costs, legal restrictions, or social custom, the potential to extend market transactions into more facets of human life appears to be substantial.

3.3 Winner-Take-All Mediation

How would digitally- mediated markets increase inequality? To the extent that digital mediation encourages a winner-take-all dynamic to extend to more areas of the economy, wealth, potentially, can be further concentrated in the hands of a small set of 'winners.' It is still in its early days, but, so far, digitally mediated markets tend to be dominated by a single company, or a few companies. If entry barriers to digital mediation were low, and if there was active competition, there would be less concern about the ability of technology companies to generate rents and capture value from others.

Companies trying to expand and defend an already dominant position in a digitally mediated market have a number of advantages: low to zero copying, storage, and transmission costs that make scaling up in size inexpensive; the network effect benefits of more users; and the network effect benefits of setting technology standards. For example, YouTube has established a dominant position in US online video, with an over 75% share of visits (Statista 2016), despite the technology to play and stream video online being fairly standard. YouTube had relatively little technological advantage initially, beyond making video uploads easier. Building on their initial user-base advantage, YouTube added additional technology features that video uploaders and users became accustomed to, making the process of video sharing a more frictionless experience. From their current position, the only realistic competition for YouTube appears to be from other giant technology companies trying to extend their offerings from other dominant positions. Possible competitors include video sharing on Facebook's dominant social media, video sales from a large hardware company like Apple, video subscriptions from Netflix, and video delivery from a large cloud computing provider such as Amazon.

Not every digitally mediated market produces one or two winners, but it is difficult to find many counter-examples. The travel market in the US is an example of increasing consolidation into three large conglomerates. However, there are still active challengers in travel niches. The expansion of 'sharing economy' Airbnb poses new competition for hotel bookings. The majority of airlines and hotels also sell through their own Internet channels. Even travel agents have not disappeared. They have been able to preserve significant market share for the older, but still active, digitally mediated market they control: the Global Distribution System. Any theory of winner-take-all digital mediation should take into account the ability to make strategic moves and countermoves.

There are also examples of alternative business models for digital mediation. In these models, more value is shared with other business models' stakeholders, and the community at large. The dominant housing rental site in the US, Craigslist, is a popular example. Run as a social enterprise, most Craigslist advertisements are free to publish.

The founder made a decision early in its life to keep the company small. Craigslist raises a relatively modest amount of revenue by charging for a few specific types of advertisements rather than seeking to maximize profits for investors or founders.

Craigslist's size and efficiency has had a measurable impact on its ability to digitally mediate. As Craigslist enters a geographic area, paid classified advertising in local newspapers declines, as does the housing vacancy rate (Kroft and Pope 2014). Estimates of the value created by Craigslist and shared with customers run into the billions of dollars. Despite attempts from heavily funded startups to compete with Craigslist directly (Brown 2014), it maintains a dominant share of many classified advertising markets in the US.

Assuming that digitally- mediated markets display winner-take-all tendencies, what are the consequences for inequality? The inequality effects appear to depend on the behavior of the institution serving as the digital mediator. It is possible to digitally mediate a market at low cost, with few people, and decide to share the value created widely rather than capture it exclusively. But few other companies have followed the Craigslist model. It could be that the founding of Craigslist was unique. The universe of people who could build a large digital marketplace, but, at the same time, are not tempted to fully capture the tremendous wealth created by it, might be small.

Alternative business models might also require technological restraint. Craigslist is a famously minimalist site with few features, relying on community members to perform labor-intensive functions such as flagging inappropriate content. The existence of alternative models for digitally mediated markets raises an important question: why is a technologically viable path—one that distributes wealth more evenly—not pursued more often in practice? Perhaps a combination of too many unique circumstances has to be in place for this apparently rare business model to survive. Perhaps it is merely untried.

Another factor in winner-take-all dynamics are the massive profits successful digital mediators are able to amass. These large cash stores do not dictate what technology companies can do, but they give companies the option of preserving their dominant position by buying out potential competitors as they arise. All of the major technology companies regularly acquire other companies. By buying the successful upstarts, even at what appear to be extremely high prices, companies can protect their entrenched position in digitally mediated markets.

3.4 Owning Exclusive Data in Mediated Markets

We live in a world of big data and massive computing power, but that does not mean data and algorithms are widely shared. Each of the two major technical capabilities discussed above, exclusive data and secretive algorithms offer powerful means for digital mediators to depart from the perfect market ideal if they so choose.

Digitally mediated markets are a major departure from the ideal of perfectly shared information. The digital mediator, in the natural course of matching buyers and sellers, acquires an incredibly detailed database of information. The database includes not only every successful transaction, but detailed information about the history of searches, stated preferences, and even unaccepted offers. These databases give the companies controlling digitally mediated markets a potential advantage in targeting offers to both buyers and sellers. It also gives digital mediators a new power of experimentation. Digitally mediated markets can flirt with different offers, fine tuning the parameters of their business models in a data-driven effort to increase value capture.

Much attention has been paid to the privacy and surveillance implications of massive consumer databases.[6] Here we are more concerned with the ability to make business models as effective as possible by capturing information about buyers, sellers, and attempts to match them. Whether the business model used in digital mediation is transaction fees, sales, subscription, or advertising, exclusive ownership of buyer data has the potential to create a powerful advantage.

For advertising, the advantages of exclusive data are many. A search history offers insight into which products or services a buyer is considering. The better targeted the advertised offer, the more likely that a willing consumer will see the advertisement and take action. Within social media, data about the extent of interaction, or engagement, with stories or posts can be used to create a detailed customer profile. The ability to combine behavioral and demographic information is particularly powerful.

Digital mediators like Google and Facebook have taken user profiling to another level. Google has more behavioral information related to product searches, but Facebook has more information submitted by users themselves about their background and interests. Facebook also knows the content users share, who their friends are, and any organizations they like. The lifeblood of the advertising business model is being able to match the right advertising messages with the right audience, and these large digital mediators have a high enough success rate to keep both advertisers and users coming back.

For a more conventional business model based on sales, a history of searches and previous purchases offers a similarly powerful capability for crafting offers. Amazon is the premier example of this, with an ongoing stream of communications to customers based on their previous searches, encouraging them to complete a transaction. Retail platforms like Amazon use recommender systems to target offers based on previously successful ones, or on offers accepted by other people with a similar profile (Adomavicius and Tuzhilin 2005). Instead of waiting for a market to discover what buyers want, the company controlling a digitally mediated market has the ability to pre-empt the sale with their own targeted offer.

The effectiveness of these techniques depends on the empirical effectiveness of targeted advertisements. Conversion rates for advertising on the Internet as a whole are low, with anywhere from 0.5 to 2% of users who see an advertisement through a Google network actually clicking on them (Irvine 2017). But with a high enough volume of visitors, and with costs per click averaging around $0.50–$2 US dollars, these advertisements are still extremely cost-effective. Other forms of advertising, such as advertising within online videos, are gaining in strength and prevalence with the large digital mediators uniquely positioned to solve the problem of advertising effectiveness. Data about buyer preferences is critical, but knowledge about the seller and products can also produce a more customized offer.

At the most basic level, markets are supposed to match buyers and sellers in an efficient, transparent way, using a relatively small amount of information. The digital mediator is the only party that possesses the database of activities and transactions. If the mediator can customize offers presented to a buyer, then this new intermediary can also experiment with the matchmaking process and with their business models. For example, exactly how much inducement does it take for a sharing economy transportation app to get more riders and drivers to use the service during off-peak times? Digital mediation provides real-time feedback on these business model decisions, and optimizing this process offers the possibility of the mediator learning the minimum amount of value that needs to be shared with each stakeholder, in any particular circumstance, to keep them participating in a business model. It allows a large company to follow the lean startup philosophy of constant experimentation and testing of their proposed business model (Ries 2011).

Almost every company can see themselves as a digital mediator, trying to match their product offerings with a universe of potential buyers. Companies have long used loyalty or reward programs to create databases about their buyers, and to track which targeted offers were successful. Loyalty programs began with banks, airlines, casinos, and grocery stores, all experimenting with different levels of inducements to learn exactly how much buyers need to be rewarded to keep their business. Why offer a free hotel room to a frequent gambler to lure them back to the casino when a cheaper steak dinner works just as well (Jeon and Hyun 2013)?

In digitally mediated markets, ownership of highly detailed exclusive data by the mediating technology company is a powerful information asymmetry. This lack of transparency is a fundamental feature of these markets, and marks a key departure from previous ideals of full transparency.

3.5 Secret Algorithms in Mediated Markets

The second new technical ability allowing a digital mediator to depart from the perfect market ideal is control over the secret algorithm matching buyers and sellers. Search engines are a prime example of a technology with a secretive, constantly changing algorithm at its center. For a single typical phrase typed into a search engine, there are millions, if not hundreds of millions, of relevant web pages containing the phrase. The search engine must select the top 10 or so results from these millions to display to a user. The algorithm converts a set of thousands, or millions, of pages into the top few pages a person will see.

If a search engine becomes an important channel for attracting customers, poor search results will cause revenue to disappear, pressuring a seller to take action to improve their search engine placement. Thus the world of search engine optimization (SEO) services came into being. Through the mysterious arts of SEO, sellers and content providers of all kinds try to reverse engineer the workings of search engine algorithms in order to appear on the all-important first few pages of results. To prevent this manipulation, the digital mediator keeps the workings of the algorithm secret. The algorithm is constantly updated to counter any new techniques found by SEO experts to 'game' the system.

In its famous search algorithm, Google assesses over 200 different factors. One of the most important factors are links from other web pages.

For example, web pages that have links from many other web pages gain reputation, which increases the likelihood of being a top search result. So, for a seller trying to game the system, an obvious strategy is to create sites linking back to your original site, or to pay others to link to your site. Once this SEO practice became widespread, Google revised its algorithm to detect and penalize this kind of 'link farming.' The Google search algorithm also gives more weight to links from sites that are older, and presumably less likely to have been created recently just to manipulate search results.

As technology evolves, new factors are added to the algorithm that separate high-quality sites from those trying to game the system. Google is now better at evaluating when sites have duplicate content and calculating which site published original content first, so that a site that copies can be penalized in the search results. Google now tracks the click-through-rate for search results, with more clicks being an indicator of higher quality search results.

Other digital mediators may start with no algorithm, or a very simple one, then evolve into a secret algorithm. A review site, for example, may begin with a simple listing of businesses in an area or category. But as the number of businesses increases, the review site switches to an algorithm to select the top search results. The algorithm is kept secret to prevent low-quality results from appearing first simply because of the skillful use of SEO tactics. The new algorithmic methods make possible new business models that take advantage of control over seller visibility.

An algorithm's lack of transparency, however, can cause problems of trust. When review sites such as Yelp use a business model of advertisements from the restaurants being reviewed, there can be the suspicion that businesses who pay for advertisements are favored in the search results (Richards 2009). Because the algorithm is secret, a digital mediator has limited options for directly proving that they do not manipulate their own results, and direct financial incentive to do so. A digital mediator can potentially benefit from control over the algorithm by promoting their own services and offers. Many of Google's battles with regulators have focused on whether Google misused their 'monopoly power' to highlight their own services in search results.

Social media is another form of digital mediation that moved from a simple timeline of all relevant updates to a secret algorithm. The Facebook news feed, itself somewhat controversial when it began, evolved from a list of updates that users had explicitly requested via friend requests and likes to a set of results controlled by the Facebook algorithm. When this change occurred, companies found their relationship with their followers went from being direct to digitally mediated. Facebook can now charge companies for access to their own followers. Social media will likely develop its own equivalent of search engine optimization as experts try to reverse engineer the secret Facebook algorithm and the commercial value of visibility on the platform grows. The digital mediators will portray themselves as neutral parties who are using the algorithm to provide the best results possible for searchers while keeping it secret to prevent bad actors from manipulating the system. The secret algorithm even gives the digital mediator a means for arguing that they, themselves, do not have complete control over the results, further reducing their responsibility for what happens on their own platforms.

These new abilities to capture value do not mean that digital mediators will necessarily do so in a way that concentrates wealth. The technology does not force mediators to share value in a certain way. But the institutional pressures on a publicly traded company, or a company with high-risk venture capital investors, encourage digital mediators to increase the value captured from their business model. As they do so, the value returned to other business model stakeholders, such as advertisers or end users, may have to be decreased. Publicly traded digital mediators are incentivized to keep their share prices up to reward the founders and early investors, to recruit new talent, and to provide a currency for acquisitions.

In summary, a useful way to analyze the new digital economy is to theorize the effects of digital technology on markets. From the dawn of the Internet era, digital technology was associated with more information sharing, better functioning markets, and the increased use of markets, but little was said about the effects of the Internet on inequality.

Instead, we see a new technology landscape which we call the 'digitally mediated market.' We identified two of the key features of mediated markets that depart from the ideal of perfect information, exclusive information, and secret algorithms, and identified some of their potential mechanisms for wealth concentration, including winner-take-all mediation and business model experimentation. The wealth-concentrating effects of mediated markets are not an inevitable outcome of digital markets, but seem to be encouraged by the business practices of digital mediators.

While the empirical evidence is not yet sufficient to claim for certain, it appears that digitally mediated markets are part of the explanation as to why digital technology and wealth inequality could co-exist, or even become more prevalent. These claims depend on features of the world that can be tested empirically: the effectiveness of targeted offerings based on exclusive data and algorithms, the goals of the organizations mediating the markets, and the institutional incentives they face. There are occasional examples of digitally mediated markets sharing value more widely, but they are rare. With digital markets sales still providing less than 10% of all retail transactions in the US (United States Census Bureau 2016), there is still plenty of room for the wealth-concentrating effects of digitally mediated markets to grow.

Notes

1. See the discussion in *The Price of Inequality* (Stiglitz 2012).
2. Stiglitz has a more complete definition of rent seeking (Stiglitz 2012).
3. See Tapscott (1996) and Kelly (1999) for prominent examples of this genre.
4. Gates was a main proponent of the 'frictionless' view of markets (Gates et al. 1995).
5. For example, the 'digital provide' of better pricing information for Kerala fisheries in Jensen (2007).
6. See the introduction and collection in Lyon (2003).

References

Adomavicius, G., & Tuzhilin, A. (2005). Toward the next generation of recommender systems: A survey of the state-of-the-art and possible extensions. *IEEE Transactions on Knowledge and Data Engineering, 17*(6), 734–749.

Bakos, Y. (1998). The emerging role of electronic marketplaces on the Internet. *Communications of the ACM, 41*(8), 35–42.

Brown, K. V. (2014). In the rental market, Craigslist may be undisruptable. Retrieved January 21, 2017, from http://www.sfgate.com/technology/article/In-the-rental-market-Craigslist-may-be-5601847.php.

Brynjolfsson, E., Malone, T. W., Gurbaxani, V., & Kambil, A. (1994). Does information technology lead to smaller firms? *Management Science, 40*(12), 1628–1644.

Fafchamps, M., & Minten, B. (2012). Impact of SMS-based agricultural information on Indian farmers. *The World Bank Economic Review, 26*(3), 383–414.

Fort, T. C., Haltiwanger, J., Jarmin, R. S., & Miranda, J. (2013). How firms respond to business cycles: The role of firm age and firm size. *IMF Economic Review, 61*(3), 520–559.

Gates, B., Myhrvold, N., & Rinearson, P. (1995). *The road ahead.* New York: Viking Penguin.

Greenwald, B. C., & Stiglitz, J. E. (1986). Externalities in economies with imperfect information and incomplete markets. *The Quarterly Journal of Economics, 101*(2), 229–264.

Irvine, M. (2017). Google AdWords benchmarks for YOUR industry [NEW DATA]. Retrieved January 26, 2017, from http://www.wordstream.com/blog/ws/2016/02/29/google-adwords-industry-benchmarks.

Jensen, R. (2007). The digital provide: Information (technology), market performance, and welfare in the South Indian fisheries sector. *The Quarterly Journal of Economics, 122*(3), 879–924.

Jeon, S. M., & Hyun, S. S. (2013). Examining the influence of casino attributes on baby boomers' satisfaction and loyalty in the casino industry. *Current Issues in Tourism, 16*(4), 343–368.

Kelly, K. (1999). *New rules for the new economy: 10 radical strategies for a connected world.* New York: Penguin.

Kim, W. C., & Mauborgne, R. (2005). *Blue ocean strategy: How to create uncontested market space and make the competition irrelevant.* Boston, MA: Harvard Business School Press.

Kroft, K., & Pope, D. G. (2014). Does online search crowd out traditional search and improve matching efficiency? Evidence from Craigslist. *Journal of Labor Economics, 32*(2), 259–303.

Luca, M. (2016). *Reviews, reputation, and revenue: The case of Yelp.com.* Retrieved from https://papers.ssrn.com/sol3/papers.cfm?abstract_id=1928601.

Lyon, D. (Ed.). (2003). *Surveillance as social sorting: Privacy, risk, and digital discrimination.* New York: Psychology Press.

Morrison, K. (2014). 81% of shoppers conduct online research before buying. Retrieved from http://www.adweek.com/socialtimes/81-shoppers-conduct-online-research-making-purchase-infographic/208527.

Porter, M. E. (2008). *Competitive strategy: Techniques for analyzing industries and competitors.* New York: Simon and Schuster.

Richards, K. (2009). Yelp and the business of extortion 2.0. Retrieved from http://www.eastbayexpress.com/oakland/yelp-and-the-business-of-extortion-20/Content?oid=1176635.

Ries, E. (2011). *The lean startup: How today's entrepreneurs use continuous innovation to create radically successful businesses.* New York: Crown Business.

Schmid, H. (2016). Should you compete with Amazon or sell on Amazon? Retrieved from https://hbr.org/2016/05/should-you-compete-with-amazon-or-sell-on-amazon.

Soper, S. (2016). More than 50% of shoppers turn first to Amazon in product search. Retrieved from https://www.bloomberg.com/news/articles/2016-09-27/more-than-50-of-shoppers-turn-first-to-amazon-in-product-search.

Statista. (2016). U.S. market share of leading multimedia websites 2016. Retrieved from https://www.statista.com/statistics/266201/us-market-share-of-leading-internet-video-portals/.

Stiglitz, J. E. (2012). *The price of inequality: How today's divided society endangers our future.* New York: W. W. Norton.

Stockdale, R., & Standing, C. (2004). Benefits and barriers of electronic marketplace participation: An SME perspective. *Journal of Enterprise Information Management, 17*(4), 301–311.

Tapscott, D. (1996). *The digital economy: Promise and peril in the age of networked intelligence.* New York: McGraw-Hill.

United States Census Bureau. (2016). Quarterly retail E-commerce sales 3rd quarter 2016 [Press release]. Retrieved from www.census.gov/retail/mrts/www/data/pdf/ec_current.pdf.

White, A., & Bodoni, S. (2016). Google unfairly curbs web ads and skews search, EU alleges. Retrieved from https://www.bloomberg.com/news/articles/2016-07-14/google-gets-eu-antitrust-complaints-on-advertising-search-iqm59p2j.

CHAPTER 4

Regulation and Taxation: The New Digital Advantage

Abstract The relationship between technology companies and aspects of their institutional context, such as regulation and taxation, is a less explored area in discussions of technology and inequality. This chapter discusses the role of intellectual property in wealth concentration, and technology companies' use of it for tax avoidance purposes. Specific forms of political lobbying, within states and in global trade regimes, are also used to help explain the wealth effects of digital technology in an era of globalization.

Keywords Information technology industry · Tax avoidance · Intellectual property · Lobbying · Globalization

4.1 Intellectual Property Wars

For digital technology companies, intellectual property rules and enforcement is a critical feature of their institutional context. Paralleling the shift from real to financial assets in household wealth, the value of assets in the largest companies has had an equally dramatic shift away from tangible assets, such as buildings and machinery, to the intangible assets of data, knowledge, reputation, and intellectual property. Intangible assets made up less than 20% of the market value of S&P 500 companies in 1975, but grew to more than 80% of asset value by 2015 (Ocean Tomo 2015). Business investment has also shifted strongly toward intangible assets over this period (Corrado and Hulten 2010). Intellectual property is a significant fraction of corporate intangible assets, particularly in the technology sector, though it is not the majority (Heitman 2016).

Two forms of intellectual property that are uniquely important for digital technology companies are patents and copyrights. The intent behind both patent and copyright protection is to create a temporary government-sanctioned monopoly that will give innovators the financial incentive to make something new and offer it to the world. The rules of intellectual property protection try to balance the societal benefits of shared innovation and creativity with the private gains inventors capture through their temporary monopolies. How, exactly, this balance is struck in the information technology sector is worthy of more attention.

Patents were originally intended to protect new and useful tangible things: physical machines, physical processes, and new materials. Natural laws and mathematical formulae were excluded from patent protection—it is not socially valuable for an individual to possess a monopoly on basic truths. Digital software, however, challenges what was previously a clear distinction between pure knowledge and its physical implementation in a machine or process. As software has become more prevalent, US courts have changed their opinion about whether computer software could be protected with patents (Cohen and Lemley 2001). At first, software was considered something close to pure mathematics, and patent applications were refused. Then, as more physical machines and processes incorporated software, patent applications began to be approved for software that happened to reside in tangible devices. Today, US courts no longer require any connection with physical devices to patent software, though the European Union still refuses to recognize software patents in most cases (González 2006).

The legitimacy of intellectual property protection in the digital world has been tested by the technologies that come closest to implementing pure mathematical algorithms. Encryption technology, for example, is basically mathematics. US law makes it illegal to decrypt a copy-protected DVD, even though decrypting a digital file is mostly the application of mathematics (Benkler 2001). Another legitimacy challenge comes from the ability to file for patent protection for business processes. Filings for business process monopolies are now not only legal in the US, they are so common they threaten to overwhelm the patent application process (Merges 1999).

The ability to patent software and business processes has raised the argument that too many obvious processes and technologies are being patented, making it too difficult for new digital inventions to arise without the permission of existing patent holders. Amazon's patent for one-click purchasing became one of the most famous examples of a potential obvious idea being patented (Dreyfuss 2000), to the detriment of all other online retailers. Another patent of the potentially obvious was issued for Priceline's 'name your own price' auctioning method, which was simply an implementation of the classic Dutch auction technique on a web site.

The legal system, through its monopoly protections, can be an effective barrier to entry, preventing entrepreneurs from challenging the status quo. The largest digital technology companies all build patent portfolios. Few of these patents generate licensing fees, the traditional way of capturing value from patents, giving rise to the 'patent paradox' of why companies spend so much money on assets that generate so little direct value (Parchomovsky and Wagner 2005). The more important function of a patent portfolio is defensive, or in deterring lawsuits from others. Larger companies have a stronger bargaining position for joint licensing negotiations if they have a large patent portfolio themselves, and are a more credible threat to sue or counter-sue. The time and costs of litigating patent suits give larger technology companies an advantage, should a patent battle ever go to court. A whole new set of companies, known to their detractors as 'patent trolls,' buy intellectual property assets for the sole purpose of extracting license fees from others (Hagiu and Yoffie 2013). This world of patent portfolios, lawsuits, and counter-suits has been described as the 'patent wars.' In the smartphone industry, for example, almost every major company is involved in multiple patent lawsuits at any one time (Segan 2012).

One might think there is a wealth concentration effect from patents and patent conflicts, especially in the technology sector. Despite the theoretical possibility of a lone entrepreneur successfully enforcing a patent against a large incumbent, patent portfolios and trolls have created an environment that gives already powerful companies a practical advantage. Companies with more resources are more likely to engage in patent lawsuits, and more likely to win. The ability to protect seemingly obvious technologies through patents, such as Apple's patents for 'slide to unlock,' or for automatically dialing a phone number on a web page, makes it harder for other companies to create new products and services in the same industry (Decker 2016). The sheer unpredictability and complexity of the legal system, with legal cases sometimes requiring multiple appeals over many years, favors the largest corporations. The counterargument is that, without patent protections, there would be less incentive to develop software. While there appears to be no shortage of software being written, it can be argued that the software industry is not as commercially successful in European and Asian jurisdictions with weaker legal protection for patents.

The second form of intellectual property uniquely important in the digital world is copyright. Copyright grants a monopoly for publishing copies of a specific, tangible work, but not the underlying ideas expressed in a work. This temporary monopoly on publication is an incentive for making creative works available to sell, even if others could copy and sell them cheaply. The digital world makes every published book, song, or video vulnerable to copying at almost zero cost, making copyright both an important legal mechanism and one that is difficult to enforce in practice.

There is a tradeoff between rewarding the authors of new work for their works, and allowing the general public to comment on, criticize, and build upon the works of others. US copyright law allows for the 'fair use' of material for educational and critical purposes, giving rights to, and creating value for, the general public. At the same time, large corporations such as Disney have successfully lobbied for copyright protections to be extended retroactively (Schlackman 2014), preserving their monopoly protections for additional decades.

For digital technologies, US copyright law is covered by the Digital Millennium Copyright Act, or DCMA, which is a complex mix of protections and restrictions. For online publishers, the DMCA provides a 'safe harbor' against copyright lawsuits (Lee 2009). Online publishers must be notified of any potential copyright violations first, then given a chance to respond before legal action can be taken against them, offering legal protection to any site accepting content from users. Without this protection, a site such as YouTube could be sued if one of their users uploaded a copyright-protected video, putting their entire business model at risk with every user contribution. However, the DMCA also makes any attempt to circumvent copy protection technology a federal crime, problematically leading to copyright protection technology that prevents any fair use of content by the general public.

The open technology movement has successfully pushed back against copyright restrictions by using a variant of copyright law itself. Free software activists have created very successful new copyright licenses that not only require the free sharing of content, but require anyone who modifies a work to share their changes with others. Thanks to these new forms of copyright, once a technology is licensed as 'open,' it stays open, giving contributors the incentive to add to a collective product, knowing that others cannot control it for their own exclusive gain. An incredible variety of open software has appeared, forming the foundation of surprisingly large community-driven projects that are used by institutions throughout the world.

Open technology projects have become so successful that they have attracted the interest of every major technology company. What began as a mostly volunteer effort is now being driven, in many cases, by contributions from large for-profit corporations (Germonprez et al. 2013). These companies see the commercial benefit of using digital technology that is built and managed by communities rather than having to develop everything themselves. The efficiency gained by letting communities decide for themselves how to build an intellectual product like software comes from what Benkler calls the economics of 'peer production.' (Benkler 2006) Peer production is uniquely powerful in the digital age, offering a new way of organizing economically valuable activity outside of both markets and corporate hierarchies. The efficiency of peer production comes from the lack of managerial overhead, but also from the motivational and knowledge benefits of allowing individuals to choose how they can best contribute to the whole.

Open movements for sharing copyright-protected content such as books, music, and public data have had more mixed success than open software. The community managed encyclopedia, Wikipedia, remains the best known example of open content, but movements to provide open educational resources such as textbooks remain small. Open content and open data movements have not yet had the same social impact as open software.

As the open software movement has shown, there can be grassroots innovation in copyright law. For intellectual property systems as a whole, however, the making of the rules, and the playing of the game, favors large corporations and government institutions. Beyond the rules themselves, however, it may be that the greatest consequence of intellectual property protections for inequality is not so much the technologies themselves, but the opportunity to rearrange tax affairs across international boundaries, where intangible corporate assets can be located anywhere in the world.

4.2 Tax Avoidance by Technology Companies

For the institutional context school, taxation policy is a major factor in wealth and income inequality. Tax codes in developed economies are famously complex, with different forms of income being taxed at a multitude of different rates. Upper-middle-class families might be the main beneficiaries of a home mortgage interest deduction, for example, while poorer families benefit from an earned income credit, and the wealthiest families are charged preferential rates for capital gains and dividends. Depending on these categorizations, the effective tax rate that wealthiest households pay may be lower than the others. In the US, this has led to the 'Buffett rule' example, with one of the country's richest billionaires paying a lower effective tax rate than his office staff (Hungerford 2011).

For individual tax payers, more layers of complexity favor those with the resources to arrange their affairs for tax avoidance opportunities. Corporate taxation, even more complex, has given rise to, and been aided by, a growing industry of accounting firms, consultancies, and legal firms dedicated to tax avoidance (Sikka and Willmott 2013), which has reached new heights in a global, multinational business environment. Corporations can choose between legal jurisdictions to find the best tax rates, or tax concessions. Tiny countries with relatively little economic activity, such as Bermuda, the Cayman Islands, and Luxembourg, becoming the headquarters for divisions of multinational firms. Larger countries also have specific methods for tax avoidance, such as the Dutch non-profit structure used by Ikea (Genschel and Schwarz 2011). Profits can be booked, or expenses declared, in the legal jurisdictions best suited to lowering a tax bill.

The scope of transnational tax avoidance is difficult to precisely calculate. The Tax Justice Network estimates that over one quarter of gross profits by US multinationals in 2012 was shifted between jurisdictions in an effort to avoid taxation (Tax Justice Network 2015), resulting in around a half a trillion US dollars per year avoiding any corporate taxation, and that amount is growing. Henry estimates that $36 trillion US of assets is currently being held in secretive offshore accounts, including

$12 trillion relocated from the developing world (Tax Justice Network 2016). If this is true, then the scope of transnational tax avoidance is likely even higher than existing estimates.

This raises the question of whether digital technology companies have any special advantage when it comes to international tax avoidance. With their significant overseas cash holdings, technology companies benefit disproportionately from international tax management, giving them the most incentive to engage in tax avoidance. But technology companies also have the fundamental advantage of their intangible assets, particularly their intellectual property. Technology companies are able to assign ownership of their intellectual property assets to a subsidiary in Ireland, Bermuda, or other jurisdictions with low corporate tax rates. The profits made through sales in higher tax countries can be shifted to lower tax countries, in the form of royalty payments for the rights to intellectual property. The parent company of Google has used a combination of entities in the Netherlands, Ireland, and Bermuda, where the intellectual property rights ultimately reside (Kahn and Drucker 2016). According to Australian journalists, curious as to why so little tax was being collected on technology sales in their country, Apple used their Ireland subsidiary to process over $100 billion in profits, paying an effective tax rate of under 0.1% (Chenoweth 2014).

Amazon benefitted from a different kind of tax advantage during its early years: the avoidance of sales tax on retail purchases. By claiming that their business had no physical presence in many US states, Amazon argued it was not obligated to collect local sales taxes. Not charging sales tax made its products cheaper for the consumer, even when Amazon's actual prices were similar to local competitors. Declaring and paying sales tax, or 'use tax,' became the responsibility of individual consumers on their annual tax returns, which, in practice, was difficult to enforce, and rarely paid (Joffe-Walt 2013). Eventually, Amazon became so large that state governments negotiated settlements directly with Amazon to automatically collect sales taxes, leveling the playing field with local businesses, but only after their initial tax advantages helped them rise to their current dominant position in online retail. In the sharing economy, Airbnb is going through a similar process. Unlike existing bed and breakfast accommodations, Airbnb, in its early days, did not collect local hotel taxes, making their products cheaper for consumers. Local governments are now pressuring Airbnb to collect local taxes.

Tax questions about digital technology companies have become controversial enough, and with high enough stakes, that political battles are breaking out at the highest levels. The European Union is insisting that Ireland charge more tax on Apple's profits, while the Irish government refuses to collect billions of euros in taxes to keep their corporate-friendly reputation. The US Treasury Department is battling American corporations that seek to relocate their headquarters overseas through foreign acquisition, a strategy known as 'tax inversion.' (Hwang 2014) Technology companies have been able to achieve similar or better reductions in taxation without a formal tax inversion, avoiding its political controversy. Local governments are more likely to be awarding tax breaks to technology companies than fighting them, hoping to lure potential employees with their high-paying jobs.

How tax policy concentrates wealth in the technology sector is worth further exploration. Technology companies have a particular ability, and motive, to shelter their profits from taxation. If large technology companies already act as wealth concentrators (for all the reasons mentioned earlier), then reducing their tax burden will only increase their contribution to rising inequality. The arguments of the institutional context school, given their fundamental assumption that technology is a tool serving human interests, accept that the business arrangement around technology is not the inevitable outcome of technology itself. Transnational taxation regimes contain within them institutional rules that can be challenged and rewritten.

4.3 State Ties and Political Lobbying by Technology Companies

Spending on corporate lobbying activity in the US has been growing faster than the size of the federal government (Drutman 2015), so it is not surprising that the digital technology sector also seeks to influence government policy. Technology companies have set aside whatever previous reputations they might have had as politically inactive to become one of the industry sectors most heavily invested in political lobbying. What began as a response to threats, such as Microsoft's responses early anti-trust lawsuits, has evolved into a view of lobbying as an opportunity to influence government policies, and implement corporate strategies (Lowery 2007).

4.3 STATE TIES AND POLITICAL LOBBYING BY TECHNOLOGY COMPANIES 69

The breadth of issues included in technology industry lobbying testifies to the complexities of their relationship to the legal environment. Tax and intellectual property law are two obvious lobbying topics, but the largest technology companies also seek to influence consumer safety law, trade policy, homeland security, immigration law, telecommunications law, labor law, and even, in the case of Amazon, aviation law for drone delivery (Orcutt 2016).

The new sharing economy companies have incorporated political influence into their corporate strategies to an even greater extent. The business model of a sharing economy company like Airbnb or Uber is not commercially viable, if the legal system classifies their activities in an unfavorable legal category. If Airbnb hosts are subject to the same regulatory restrictions and taxation as hotels, their business model cannot function. The same applies if Uber drivers are classified as employees rather than independent contractors, or if taxi regulations are enforced.

It was vital for Uber and Lyft lobbyists to help create new legal categories, such as the Transportation Network Company created by the California Public Utilities Commission in 2013, that would make a more favorable regulatory environment for their businesses (Geron 2013). Because many of these regulations are controlled by local governments, sharing economy startups had to develop a real strength in local government lobbying to meet their ambitious growth targets. These companies learned how to combine a surge in lobbying activities with public relations strategies, such as galvanizing drivers and customers to gather for local government hearings, while at the same time launching their services without regard for existing regulations (Weise 2015).

Technology companies are more subject to legal ambiguity than many others, as innovations create new legal situations that do not perfectly match previous case law. For example, privacy regulations that assume government surveillance requires a physical search do not apply to situations where every Internet data packet can easily be monitored and stored. In legal systems based on precedent, every technological advance opens the possibility of a new law or ruling.

The fates of digital technology companies are also closely connected to public resources, further entangling the technology sector in legal issues. Public resources are critical for networking infrastructure, including electromagnetic spectrum, and rights of way for cables and radio towers. Regulations determine the cost of infrastructure, and their rules of access and use, in ways that make new business models more or less viable. Less directly, technology companies require an educated workforce, whose cost and quality are determined by education and immigration policy.

Attempts to influence also move in the opposite direction. With digital technology companies becoming wealthy and powerful, governments seek to influence corporations that can further a state's economic and even military strategies. Nation states can influence the fate of their 'national champions' by restricting what they define as military technology, using veto power over mergers and acquisitions, purchasing power, and by insisting on open access to foreign technology.

Mass surveillance is one area where nation states have been effective in persuading digital technology companies to cooperate closely. The recent Yahoo! revelations show at least one example of a technology company providing a general search capability for all emails and messages to a US intelligence agency (Menn 2016). The temptation of monitoring every communication is too great for governments to pass up. The US government can bring surveillance requests to the Foreign Intelligence Surveillance Court, a secret tribunal. Technology companies are prevented by law from revealing the details of these surveillance requests, but are reporting on their frequency. National surveillance systems of the Internet in Iran, China, and other countries also demand the cooperation of technology companies for their implementation (Powers and Jablonski 2015).

Government ties with the technology industry potentially impact wealth inequality, but what are those effects? Though direct evidence is lacking, it is reasonable to assume that complex government regulations would favor larger companies with more resources over smaller upstarts. To the extent that new business models require new laws or regulations to be viable, lobbying and government regulations would be a real barrier to entry for any entrepreneur. The case of Uber shows that a startup can manage this process to their advantage, in part by making government lobbying a core strategic capability. This approach only worked, however, with the backing of hundreds of millions of dollars in venture capital, which brings its own pressures to maximize value capture for groups who are already wealthy. The wealth effects of government surveillance are not as clear. Perhaps a smaller company, or an organization with a non-profit or alternative business model, could sneak in under the radar and not be targeted by government surveillance requests.

However, the few startups that have tried to offer services immune to government surveillance have faced obvious legal difficulties.

4.4 Technology-Driven Globalization and Trade Regimes

Digital technology has long been associated with globalized trade. Digital infrastructure provides the material basis for redistributing work across geographic boundaries, and also across legal and regulatory boundaries as well. Once global fiber optic networks are in place, any location connected to the Internet can access distant labor and skills.

The extent to which work can be digitally transferred to a distant location depends in part of the nature of the work itself. If the work requires access to data, or the ability to communicate, digital capabilities can make those job functions mobile. Radiologists in India, for example, could examine a Canadian X-ray, or a programmer in Poland could write a software module for a German company. If the work is partially or wholly automatable through software, then distant labor might become a substitute for local labor. Employees in the Philippines, for example, could be used to staff an American call center. With full automation, however, an overseas call center might be replaced completely by cloud software, so the effects of technological capabilities can vary.

Large technology companies have taken advantage of global trade to distribute work around the world. Data centers and business processes are commonly outsourced from developed economies to developing ones. This outsourcing often uses a complex mixture of outsourced services, in-house expertize, and more fully automated cloud-based services rather than a simple shipment of whole areas of activity overseas (Rivard and Aubert 2015). Large technology companies possess networks of research and development facilities around the world, using engineering talent from specific regions. There is an extensive body of research on how and when corporations decide to outsource globally, but little recent research on the effect of outsourcing on jobs.

The new world of cross-border digital trade has also manifested itself in the new markets for global freelance talent. The image of 'digital nomads,' able to work anywhere in the world with Internet access while enjoying attractive leisure lifestyles, offers a positive, empowered view of global freelancing (Richards 2015). The reality of global freelance markets for most overseas labor appears to be extreme price competition, openly discriminatory behavior, and difficulty in charging more for higher skills and expertize (Beerepoot and Lambregts 2015). As of today, these freelance markets are too small to have had a significant effect on wealth inequality.

Ultimately, it may be that the most significant effect of globalization for wealth inequality is through regulatory arbitrage. Regulatory arbitrage is the ability to choose which country's legal and regulatory framework is the most advantageous for a corporation or individual (Riles 2014). It would be disappointing if the main revolutionary potential of digital technology was simply to escape regulations, but early Internet commentators celebrated the idea that digital technology was beyond the control of any one nation state, with Gilmore famously claiming the Internet would consider censorship as 'damage' and simply route data around it (Goldsmith and Wu 2006). National surveillance programs have dented these extreme views of state helplessness in the face of digital technology, but globalization has certainly allowed a wider variety of jurisdictional choices for locating business activities. The differences in tax regimes discussed in previous sections are important, but labor and environmental laws may be even more important factors in work offshoring decisions.

Living in a 'flat' world does not guarantee that digital technology will have a uniform effect around the globe. Digital infrastructure is still unevenly distributed. Fiber optic networks, computers, and the skills needed to use technology to its fullest are expensive. Freely flowing information through the Internet is not a given, and neither is the equal treatment of all businesses.

In conclusion, it is difficult to summarize the arguments of the institutional context school because of their diversity. In general, institutional context claims economic rules and regulations are the main drivers of inequality, and that digital technology is at best a tool, or enabler, of change, and a fairly generic one at that. The institutional context message can be seen as uplifting, in the sense that greater inequality might be caused by human choices, which can always be changed, rather than technological forces beyond our control, but that simplified view downplays the inertia behind institutions such as legal and regulatory regimes. By definition, institutions are systems of behavior that endure, and institutional change is not an easy task. The focus on economic and political rules also leaves out the whole dynamic of technology decision-making, and their subsequent effects on behaviors that become entrenched, and unexamined. A strength of the institutional context school, however, lies in the clear lines of causality from a situation infused with digital technology to a distribution of wealth. It is very clear how tax rules, or the value of intellectual property, contribute to wealth inequality.

Both the technological and the institutional context schools suffer from an emphasis on the presence or absence of explanatory factors, rather than the process of change. In the classic distinction between explanations that use factors, versus explanations that use processes (Markus and Robey 1988), recent scholarship in business and technology has leaned toward identifying the practices through which technology is designed, used, and, ultimately, has an effect on the world. Explanations based on process have a better chance of leading to meaningful actions and prescriptions for change because process explanations address issues under the control of participants rather than abstract factors that often are not (Ramiller and Pentland 2009). In the next chapter, we are tasked with theorizing the key processes involved in technology and inequality, in which we attempt to integrate both the technological and institutional context schools through specific processes of designing, deploying, and using technology.

References

Beerepoot, N., & Lambregts, B. (2015). Competition in online job marketplaces: Towards a global labour market for outsourcing services? *Global Networks, 15*(2), 236–255.

Benkler, Y. (2001). The battle over the institutional ecosystem in the digital environment. *Communications of the ACM, 44*(2), 84–84.

Benkler, Y. (2006). *The wealth of networks: How social production transforms markets and freedom*. New Haven, CT: Yale University Press.

Chenoweth, N. (2014). How Ireland got Apple's $9bn profit. Retrieved January 29, 2017, from http://www.afr.com/news/politics/national/how-ireland-got-apples-9bn-profit-20140305-j7cxm.

Cohen, J. E., & Lemley, M. A. (2001). Patent scope and innovation in the software industry. *California Law Review, 89*(1), 1–57.

Corrado, C. A., & Hulten, C. R. (2010). How do you measure a "technological revolution"? *The American Economic Review, 100*(2), 99–104.

Decker, S. (2016). Apple wins appeal reinstating $119.6 million Samsung verdict. Retrieved January 27, 2017, from https://www.bloomberg.com/news/

articles/2016-10-07/apple-wins-appeal-reinstating-119-6-million-samsung-verdict.

Dreyfuss, R. C. (2000). Are business method patents bad for business. *Santa Clara Computer & High Technology Law Journal, 16*, 263.

Drutman, L. (2015). *The business of America is lobbying: How corporations became politicized and politics became more corporate*. New York: Oxford University Press.

Genschel, P., & Schwarz, P. (2011). Tax competition: A literature review. *Socio-Economic Review, 9*(2), 339–370.

Germonprez, M., Allen, J., Warner, B., Hill, J., & McClements, G. (2013). Open source communities of competitors. *Interactions, 20*(6), 54–59.

Geron, T. (2013). California becomes first state to regulate ridesharing services Lyft, Sidecar, UberX. Retrieved January 30, 2017, from http://www.forbes.com/sites/tomiogeron/2013/09/19/california-becomes-first-state-to-regulate-ridesharing-services-lyft-sidecar-uberx/ - 61d6dbd767fe.

Goldsmith, J., & Wu, T. (2006). *Who controls the Internet?: Illusions of a borderless world*. New York: Oxford University Press.

González, A. G. (2006). The software patent debate. *Journal of Intellectual Property Law & Practice, 1*(3), 196–206.

Hagiu, A., & Yoffie, D. B. (2013). The new patent intermediaries: Platforms, defensive aggregators, and super-aggregators. *The Journal of Economic Perspectives, 27*(1), 45–65.

Heitman, W. (2016). Intangible assets: They're not what you think they are. http://ww2.cfo.com/accounting/2016/07/intangible-assets-theyre-not-think/.

Hungerford, T. L. (2011). An analysis of the "Buffett Rule". Retrieved January 28, 2017, from http://digitalcommons.ilr.cornell.edu/key_workplace/865/?utm_source=digitalcommons.ilr.cornell.edu%2Fkey_workplace%2F865&utm_medium=PDF&utm_campaign=PDFCoverPages.

Hwang, C. (2014). The new corporate migration: Tax diversion through inversion. *Brooklyn Law Review, 80*, 807.

Joffe-Walt, C. (2013). Most people are supposed to pay this tax. Almost nobody actually pays it. Retrieved January 29, 2017, from http://www.npr.org/sections/money/2013/04/16/177384487/most-people-are-supposed-to-pay-this-tax.

Kahn, J., & Drucker, J. (2016). Google lowered taxes by $2.4 billion using European subsidiaries. Retrieved January 29, 2017, from https://www.bloomberg.com/news/articles/2016-02-19/google-lowered-taxes-by-2-4-billion-using-european-subsidiaries.

Lee, E. (2009). Decoding the DMCA safe harbors. *Columbia Journal of Law & the Arts, 32*, 233–276.

Lowery, D. (2007). Why do organized interests lobby? A multi-goal, multi-context theory of lobbying. *Polity, 39*(1), 29–54.

Markus, M. L., & Robey, D. (1988). Information technology and organizational change: Causal structure in theory and research. *Management Science, 34*(5), 583–598.

Menn, J. (2016). Exclusive: Yahoo secretly scanned customer emails for U.S. intelligence—sources. Retrieved January 30, 2017, from http://www.reuters.com/article/us-yahoo-nsa-exclusive-idUSKCN1241YT.

Merges, R. P. (1999). As many as six impossible patents before breakfast: Property rights for business concepts and patent system reform. *Berkeley Technology Law Journal*, 577–615.

Ocean Tomo. (2015). Annual study of intangible asset market value from Ocean Tomo, LLC. Retrieved January 27, 2017, from http://www.oceantomo.com/2015/03/04/2015-intangible-asset-market-value-study/.

Orcutt, M. (2016). Tech giants go to Washington. Retrieved January 30, 2017, from https://www.technologyreview.com/s/602172/tech-giants-go-to-washington/.

Parchomovsky, G., & Wagner, R. P. (2005). Patent portfolios. *University of Pennsylvania Law Review, 154*(1), 1–77.

Powers, S. M., & Jablonski, M. (2015). *The real cyber war: The political economy of internet freedom*. Urbana, IL: University of Illinois Press.

Ramiller, N. C., & Pentland, B. T. (2009). Management implications in information systems research: The untold story. *Journal of the Association for Information Systems, 10*(6), 474.

Richards, G. (2015). The new global nomads: Youth travel in a globalizing world. *Tourism Recreation Research, 40*(3), 340–352.

Riles, A. (2014). Managing regulatory arbitrage: A conflict of laws approach. *Cornell International Law Journal, 47*, 63.

Rivard, S., & Aubert, B. A. (Eds.). (2015). *Information technology outsourcing*. London: Routledge.

Schlackman, S. (2014). How Mickey Mouse keeps changing copyright law. Retrieved January 27, 2017, from http://artlawjournal.com/mickey-mouse-keeps-changing-copyright-law/.

Segan, S. (2012). Infographic: Smartphone patent wars explained. Retrieved January 27, 2017, from http://www.pcmag.com/article2/0,2817,2399098,00.asp.

Sikka, P., & Willmott, H. (2013). The tax avoidance industry: Accountancy firms on the make. *Critical Perspectives on International Business, 9*(4), 415–443.

Tax Justice Network. (2015). The scale of base erosion and profit shifting (BEPS). Retrieved January 29, 2017, from http://www.taxjustice.net/scaleBEPS/.

Tax Justice Network. (2016). More than $12 trillion stuffed offshore, from developing countries alone. Retrieved January 29, 2017, from http://www.taxjustice.net/2016/05/09/17103/.

Weise, K. (2015). This is how Uber takes over a city. Retrieved January 30, 2017, from https://www.bloomberg.com/news/features/2015-06-23/this-is-how-uber-takes-over-a-city.

CHAPTER 5

Models, Mediation, and Mobilization: A Framework for Analyzing Technology and Inequality

Abstract This chapter builds a simple conceptual framework for analyzing technology and inequality, bringing together aspects of both the technological and institutional context schools. Drawing from the Science and Technology Studies (STS) literature, the framework begins with a 'practice' view of technological systems, including technology practice (how technology choices are embedded in specific artifacts and processes), and business practice (how business model choices lead to specific value creation and capture activities). The conceptual framework draws attention to how technology *mediation*, the business *model*, and the *mobilization* of key stakeholders affect the creation and capture of value, leading to shifts in wealth or *wealth effects*. Figure 5.1 provides a graphic overview of the conceptual framework.

Keywords History of technology · Sociology of technology Technological mediation · Value creation · Value capture Business models

5.1 Technology Business Models

At the heart of our conceptual framework for tracing the impacts of technology and inequality is the business *model*.[1] Originally developed in the strategy and entrepreneurship academic literatures, the business model idea is commonly used in the technology sector. A business model

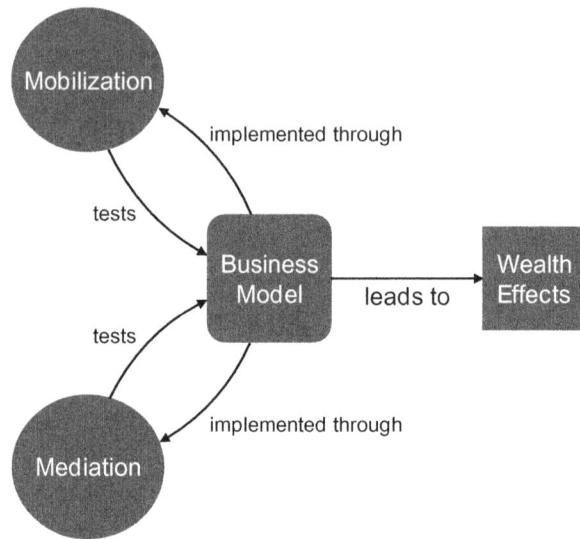

Fig. 5.1 The conceptual framework: business model, mediation, mobilization, and wealth effects

describes a unique combination of resources, processes, and relationships that creates value, captures that value, and shares that value among stakeholders. The business model, in effect, acts as a proposal for how value will be created and captured, and is a tool for analysis, understanding, and planning rather than a physical thing. Though the concept is well-grounded in academic literature, it is rare that an academic concept also be widely used by practitioners in the field (Fig. 5.1).

The Osterwalder and Pigneur (2010) framework offers a popular definition of the different components of a business model. At the center of the business model is the customer value proposition, a hypothesis predicting the benefit the end customer will derive from a product or service. The business model describes the relationships needed to produce and distribute the intended customer value, and these relationships are critical—especially for digital products and services—because no single company or group will ever create every aspect of hardware, software, and global networking on their own. The business model also describes the resources needed to deliver on the customer value proposition, including technology, information, and processes. Their framework highlights how digital technology and information have become key resources for value creation and capture in many business models, and their business model 'canvas' invites analysts to imagine how digital technologies enable alternative business models, either through new sources of value creation, or simply by offering new forms of value capture.

The key conceptual point is that a business model is an analytic tool (Teece 2010). It is a theory, or hypothesis, about how disparate things and processes can hold together to create a business that can last. As a hypothesis, a business model exists to be tested, and modified. It changes the emphasis in business strategy and entrepreneurship from efficient production to effective experimentation. It brings an empirical, almost scientific mindset to business that is very different from previous generations of management science, which applied mathematical formulae to pre-defined production problems. It is a search for what works in a complex world. Those who are better equipped for the search will be more likely to find new business models, improve them, and move on to a different model when situations change.

As with any hypothesis, there are many different ways a business model can be wrong. The customer value proposition may not be as attractive as predicted. It may not be possible to create the value anticipated by the business model because some of the predictions about who and what is necessary to produce value are not correct. Stakeholders or resources may not perform at the predicted level, or they may not participate in the business model at all. The predicted value might be created successfully, only to find that the value cannot be sufficiently captured.

Digital technology companies have been at the forefront of the search for new business models. The online world, with its global access and near-zero copying costs, is a challenging environment for the traditional business model of product sales. A traditional business model for content industries would be to sell books, music, or newspapers through physical distribution channels. These business models are being severely challenged. Newspapers have seen their lucrative classified advertising business disappear, replaced by online platforms such as Craigslist. Newspaper subscriptions have significantly declined because of competition from free news content online. The music industry is shifting to subscription-based service, with customers congregating in the few available online platforms, such as Spotify and Apple, that are large enough to negotiate access to comprehensive music catalogs; or, music is being given away as a kind of marketing expense to attract other business, such as live performances. With physical book sales declining, but e-book sales rising (Gilbert 2015), new consumer behaviors are emerging that combine physical bookstores, with their tactile experience and more serendipitous discoveries, and online bookstores, with their greater inventory and more focused consumer search behavior (Laing and Royle 2013).

A wide variety of new business models for digital content are currently being tested. There is the traditional display advertising model, but it faces challenges from ad blocking technology when content is consumed through open channels, such as web browsers. Companies have experimented with freemium models, providing free levels of access and charging for premium services, but the uptake of premium services is punishingly low unless there are a wide variety of service options that match the different commitment levels and preferences of consumers (Seufert 2013). Companies such as Apple use an integrated hardware business model, making access to their software dependent on buying their expensive physical products. Facebook, despite its ubiquity and extreme popularity with users, does not offer subscriptions, preferring an advertising-based business model.

The digital world can breathe new life into existing business models like advertising. Social media platforms can boost advertising effectiveness by accessing detailed demographic information from user profiles and behavioral information about how their users interact with content. Search engines have also pursued an almost entirely advertising-based business model, using their unique information about search engine queries, and online activities tracked through web and mobile analytics, to improve advertising effectiveness.

Business models can evolve and combine over time. Google has moved into providing operating systems for mobile and hardware devices, which is closer to an Apple hardware model, in order to preserve direct access to users and their behavioral data. Microsoft has moved toward offering their software as cloud-based services, bundling software with infrastructure such as computing power and storage, and charging a subscription fee. As we can see, constant experimentation with business models is the rule in digital industries.

In online commerce, Amazon has maintained the traditional business model of selling goods, but has added many new twists by opening up their business as a platform for others. Third parties can use Amazon's digital platform, and Amazon will fulfill product orders from their warehouse; and Amazon's lucrative new business model opens their computing infrastructure to outside users. Their cloud-based computing and storage services, Amazon Web Services, have become the largest source of cloud infrastructure for other companies and entrepreneurs, helping new entrants in digital product and service markets scale up more efficiently.

A business model is supposed to be experimental. It is a hypothesis of how value creation and capture will work. The role of the company, or entrepreneur, is to constantly test the model against reality, and adjust or abandon as necessary. This view is consistent with the lean startup philosophy of Ries, Blank, and other theorists of high-technology entrepreneurship, who see startups as the search for an effective business model.[2] The experimental aspect adds a dynamism to the digital technology sector, which will be the key to our understanding of technology and business. Having the right digital resources gives technology companies an advantage in finding sustainable new business models, and for perfecting the business model that can maximize value capture. But knowledge is never perfect. Situations change, and there are many moving parts, so the creation of a business model and fitting it against reality is a constant effort, with many possibilities for disconnection.

A weakness of the business model concept, as it has been used in entrepreneurship and strategy, is its downplaying the difficulty of execution. The approach tends to assume that design is the tough job, compared to the work of keeping partners and customers on board, technologies working as they are supposed to, and resources acquired and deployed skillfully. Maintaining a focus on the experimental aspects of business models helps keep this conceptual weakness in check.

5.2 Technology Mediation

The second concept in our framework is technology mediation. Technology mediation is a set of specific technological choices about how to mediate people and the world. How do choices about the best way to represent reality in the digital realm, including both human relationships and physical things, make a difference in the real world?

To answer this question, we can draw upon a sophisticated body of scholarship that has taken on the question of how technology affects the world. Technology is paradoxical, in the sense that it is intended to give humanity control over the physical world, yet also, to some degree, remains outside human control. Technology harnesses knowledge of the natural world; the natural world is outside of our control, and our knowledge of it is never perfect. Technology, therefore, may work as its designers intend, or it may not.

Technological evolution can increase our ability to control the natural world. But, like nuclear weapons and bioengineered viruses in real life, or Frankenstein and Skynet in popular culture, creating is not the same as controlling. There is a recurring theme in the study of human technology of creating powerful things, without, necessarily, the wisdom required to use them properly. Taken to the extreme, technology provides the ultimate power, the power to destroy our own species, and our own planet, and its effects need to be analyzed as we have to choose between, or figure out how to move between, both the in-control and out-of-control aspects of technology.

The two basic schools of thought about technology and inequality, what we have called the technological school and the institutional context school, correspond to two basic philosophical positions used in the analysis of technology. Technology can be seen as a force, or an independent cause of change humanity reacts to, such as when the inherent skill requirements of a new technology cause changes in work, the logic of technological determinism viewing technology as a force causing social change. Or technology can be seen as a tool, an instrument that reflects and implements human choices, such as when digital technology is used as a means for regulatory avoidance by relocating work around the world.

In academic fields devoted to the history, sociology, and philosophy of technology, we find many theoretical attempts to describe technology that transcend this simple distinction between force and tool. We will summarize three other philosophical positions that provide a level of nuance beyond the reductive views of technology as either a force of nature, or a tool created by humans. These three positions are technology as 'history,' technology as 'values,' and technology as 'practice.'

Technology as history recognizes that technology choices and commitments are made over time, and these commitments are not equally easy to reverse later. Economists refer to investments and sunk costs, such as investments in roads, oil pipelines, and refineries that change the attractiveness of fossil fuel technology, for example, versus other energy sources. These investments in some ways place technology outside of our control as an independent cause of human action, leading most people to continue to use fossil fuels for transportation, even though they reflect human choices made in the past. Investments in technology standards, such as the QWERTY keyboard in English language countries, survive more because of past commitments to training and software rather than because of any sense of technological superiority. The Actor-Network Theory tradition of technological analysis argues that past modifications to physical reality, such as speed bumps on a road, can take the place of human presence, such as a highway patrol, as a 'force' affecting human behavior, such as whether they drive at excessive speeds (Latour 2005). At specific moments in time, according to this position, technology is more open to change than others. Technology as history understands technology as a force varying in its strength over time due to past commitments and social relations.

The technology as values agrees that technology is a tool that reflects human choices, but does not assume all humans share the same goals or intentions for a certain technology. In the Social Construction of Technology tradition of technological analysis, a technology cannot be understood independent of its success criteria, or what problem it is trying to solve. In extreme cases, technologies that appear to be nonsensical make sense when certain values are understood. To take a famous example, nineteenth century penny-farthing bicycles, with their huge front wheels, seem obviously inferior to modern safety bicycles. But if an important objective of bicycles is to demonstrate the bravery of their young male riders, a less safe but faster bicycle is the better solution (Bijker et al. 1987). A technology may be made of hard materials, but its success is always dependent on human values, and how it achieves them. If those values are contested, as they were when more safety-minded bicycle riders (and sellers) wanted to shift the solution criteria to a technology with a broader social and market appeal, then the tool perspective needs to be complemented with an understanding of the process through which technological values are defined.

The technology as practice perspective argues that technology is only brought into being, and used, as a result of systematic human behavior. Technology may appear to be a force that affects humanity from the outside world, but that force only manifests itself through human action. In the most extreme case, even the ability to build and operate a nuclear weapon—the ultimate case of the genie that allegedly cannot be put back into the bottle—could be lost if the next generation of engineers loses the highly specialized skills necessary to keep nuclear weapons operating (MacKenzie and Spinardi 1995). By way of correcting the tool perspective, the practice view highlights the classic disconnect between what designers intend and what technology actually does. In the digital world, error-free software does not exist; there are too many different input combinations to feasibly test every possibility for anything larger than the most trivial technology (Myers et al. 2011). Designers may not understand the needs of the people who use a technology (Courage and Baxter 2005), they may not be able to anticipate all future circumstances, or may simply lack the knowledge and skill to achieve their intention. Technology depends on skillful operation and maintenance, which may not occur. Another way to look at the disconnect is to think of designers as writing a script, or a role for technology to play in a larger system, and the technology successfully or unsuccessfully playing that role as written (Akrich 1992).

In this work, we will draw on all three of these philosophical positions, with particular emphasis on the practice view, as we describe digital mediation in our conceptual framework through the use of technological mediation theory. Following Verbeek (2015), we can think of technologies as attempts to implement behavioral scripts, both the behavior of the technology, and the behavior of the people who interact with it. Technologies, particularly digital technologies, mediate a number of different relationships. Technology mediates the relationship between a human and the world, such as when a new device, like a microscope, or a complex assembly of devices and software, like an inventory control system, allows a person to see aspects of the world they could not see otherwise. The technology in these cases might be experienced as tools to be used for human ends, but mediation theory argues that technology always provides a limited view of the world, representing reality in a way that highlights certain aspects, often deliberately and usefully so, and downplaying others.

As a technology that can perform actions on its own, as well as provide information to others, digital technology affects both human action and perception. Verbeek defines the design of technology as the deliberate insertion of behavioral scripts into technology addressing both perception and action. Perception choices result in either *amplification* or *reduction* of certain kinds of information. Action choices result in either an *invitation* to perform certain kinds of behaviors, or an *inhibition* against them.

In technological mediation theory, technologies also represent, and stand between, human relationships. Buyers and sellers in online marketplaces rate and review each other. Social media defines networks of friends and followers, each with their own rules for interaction and communication. Along the way, there are many mediation choices about how to represent human relationships. For example, what preference is given to seeing updates from friends versus commercial entities? What happens when content is 'liked'? How does this change the flow of information in a news feed? What kinds of direct communications are possible between friends versus those who lack a connection?

Perception and action choices affect human interaction and communication, and one of those effects is stability. A technology becomes stable when the technology, and the people interacting with it, are able to play their scripted roles consistently, achieving an outcome defined as successful by the context surrounding it. As noted by the values view of technology, the definition of success is not inherent in the technology itself. Mediation theory calls this 'multistability,' or the ability of a technological artifact to evolve into different technologies when used in practice. Verbeek uses the example of the telephone, which began as a hearing aid, but later became a general purpose communication device (Verbeek 2006). History is full of similar examples of technologies that were supposed to be used in one way, and became used for another.[3]

Mediation theory views technology as a kind of applied ethics. Technology designers make decisions with an intent to influence human behavior and worldviews. Technological mediation offers new possibilities for action, and therefore new moral decisions.[4] In this theory, the influence of technology on human action varies along two different dimensions: visibility and force. The visibility of influence can be either *apparent* or *hidden*. The force of influence can be either *strong* or relatively *weak*. A technology with a strong and apparent influence is called 'coercive,' for example, a breath tester for alcohol attached to a car ignition; a weak but openly apparent influence is called 'persuasive,' for example, a fitness tracking device worn on a wrist. Hidden influence, which Verbeek calls 'decisive,' can also be strong while a weak, hidden influence is called 'seductive.'

Mediation theory provides a vocabulary for talking about the influence of technology on action and perception, but it does not explain how a particular mediation came to be. The classic theory implicitly assumes a single designer who intends to build a script in and around technology. The reality of technology design practice, at least for commercially available technologies, includes a far more diverse set of individuals and circumstances. Real technologies have a history, or a set of commitments over time. They reflect multiple values, and involve designers, operators, maintainers, and users within multiple practice traditions. This is why mediation is used as just one aspect of our overall conceptual framework, and to describe one of the two most important means for implementing and testing a business model. The other important means, mobilizing the support of other groups, is discussed in the next section.

5.3 Technology Mobilization

To implement and test most digital business models, multiple parties need to play their respective roles. The effects of technology are dependent on how these parties are mobilized. In technology studies, mobilization is used to describe the techniques that maintain the cooperation and involvement of all the parties necessary for a technology to succeed. Customers need to be aware of the value proposition, accept it, and often times perform activities themselves to help realize the value of it for themselves. Partners need to be kept on board, such as the app developers for an app store. Investors need to be attracted, as do skilled employees. In some models, regulators and community members may also be important constituents.

Mobilization processes can be theorized in different ways, but one of the most intriguing is to consider technology deployment as being analogous to a social movement (Elliott and Kraemer 2008). According to this theory, successful technologies are those that create a compelling vision and then mobilize the right people around that vision. The vision's characteristics, then, are very important. Visions may promise larger social changes, or relatively narrow technical or economic benefits. They may only specify a problem that needs to be rectified, or they might propose a specific solution to those problems. There can be tradeoffs between visions that are more inclusive, but vague, as opposed to visions that are more specific in their remedies, but appeal to fewer people.

Another aspect of mobilization are the risk and reward tradeoffs for different groups. For any new business model, one must ask what the risk of moving away from their previous ways of doing things is, and determine how much of an incentive or reward they will receive for doing it. Other questions that might be asked: How does a business model share the value jointly created by all parties while still keeping everyone participating? Who needs the largest inducements, and who will be satisfied with less? For example, two-sided markets that have to attract both buyers and sellers have the option of subsidizing one side versus the other, depending on whether buyers or sellers are more difficult to attract. A ride-sharing platform needs to balance the needs of drivers for higher income with the desires of consumers for cheaper fares. Money is often a prime consideration in mobilization around a technology business model, but is not the only one. Time, enjoyment, status, and many other issues can come into play. Mobilization includes any tactics or commitments that will keep a group playing a certain role in a business model.

Popular definitions of business models, such as Osterwalder and Pigneur's, offer generic parties that can be included in an analysis of mobilization. Using their definition, a focal company or organization keeps a business model together, and the customer value proposition acts as the vision that retains the cooperation of customers and end users of a technology, defining the role every party plays in exchanges, whether it involves paying money, contributing time, or sharing valuable data. Generic types of actors to be mobilized include customers and users, suppliers, and partners.

Regulators and investors are two other generic types who may be important, depending on the specific business model. If a business model is not self-funded through customer revenue, investors will have to be kept on board. Investors will need to see either loan payments or equity values that meet their expectations. For non-publically traded technology companies, equity value is more speculative, perhaps depending more on public perception than anything else.

Meeting the expectations of investors to keep cooperation can drive changes in the business model. In Uber's case, for example, a startup trying to maintain their multi-billion US dollar valuation, current profits or customer revenue may not be as important as the credibility or excitement of the growth story embedded in their vision. To meet these expectations, their business model might react by including other business ideas, such as food delivery or autonomous vehicles, as a signal to investors that the business model is larger than a simple transportation app, but these changes in vision may have implications for other aspects of the business model.

Digital business model investors, particularly early-stage investors and venture capitalists who specialize in high-growth technology companies, have specific return expectations that encourage business models to pursue high risk and high growth. To mobilize these investors, a customer value proposition needs to serve large markets. Once the companies are larger and more established, like a Google or a Microsoft, the expectations of early high-risk investors fade in importance compared to other parties. Large technology companies have techniques at their disposal for insulating themselves against some forms of investor pressure, such as creating classes of equity shares with different voting rights. However, if executive bonuses and new employee compensation depend on share price, then the mobilization strategies of even the largest technology companies can be affected by stock market prices and perceptions.

No one corporation or institution, even the largest, can operate a major digital technology enterprise completely on their own. Hardware producers, such as Apple, need subcontractors and partners, and corporate software developers, like Microsoft, need sales-channel partners, partnerships that are normal for any large corporation. What is, perhaps, unique in the digital world is the extent to which customers have to contribute. For a search engine to have value, a whole universe of web pages needs to be created, maintained, and freely shared. For a social media platform to have value, users must contribute billions of status updates and photos. Digital hardware and software producers rely on open source software communities and open standards for their products and services. Keeping customers mobilized and contributing not just as buyers, but as active and willing participants, is a key challenge.

5.4 Technology, Value Capture, and Wealth Shifts

In our simple conceptual framework, *mediation*, *model*, and *mobilization* affect the distribution of wealth. The business model leads to shifts in wealth that increase or decrease inequality through its processes of value creation and value capture. Taking into consideration only the shifts in equity value in the largest technology companies, combined with their large profits, dividends, share buybacks, and cash holdings, the technology sector can directly account for multiple trillions of US dollars in wealth shifts, enough to be significant for the entire economy. If digital technology plays a role in other wealth shifts, such as the approximately 5% of US GDP that has shifted from wages to corporate profits since 1980, or the tens of trillions of US dollars kept in secretive offshore accounts, then the potential impact of technology is even larger. Any repeat of these trends in other countries would make the impact even more significant.

The business models powerful enough to generate these kind of wealth shifts include traditional sales of products and services in the information technology industry. Digital hardware sales can have high profit margins, but what is more revealing is the breakdown of the value captured by different participants (Linden et al. 2009). For each of the early Apple iPods sold, only $40 of value was captured by the many companies who provide components and manufacturing services, most of which went to technology suppliers in Japan, Taiwan, and the US. The companies in China that assembled the devices captured, at most, a few dollars out of that $40. Apple alone captured $80 of value per iPod sold, twice as much as every other party. Another $75 of value was captured by the distribution and retail channel in the US that sold the device, which might be Apple itself if the iPod was purchased at an Apple store or web site. Not all digital hardware devices have a profit margin as large as Apple's early music players, but this example shows that the company coordinating the business model, bringing all the other players together, can capture a substantial fraction of the value created.

Digital software sales can generate even higher profit margins than hardware. Software can be built on a foundation of existing technology, by relatively small groups of people, and copied and distributed globally for minimal cost. For a company like Microsoft, an 80–90% gross profit margin for their software divisions is not unusual, while margins in their hardware divisions might be 20–30% or less.[5] For digital businesses that depend on public resources, such as electromagnetic spectrum, or rights of way for fiber optic cables, the resulting monopolies or duopolies can be highly profitable depending on the way these resources are regulated. Despite being the home of many large technology companies, Internet access is generally slower and more expensive in major US cities than their European or Asian counterparts (Russo et al. 2014), possibly leading to larger profits.

As we move away from the traditional business models of selling technology products and services, impressively high profits in the newer digital business models are possible. In electronic commerce, Amazon has been able to consolidate and capture almost 50% of all online retail sales in the US, taking advantage of their unique customer data and their marketplace access to sell goods themselves, and provide services to potential competitors who sell through their platform. Business models based on advertising, used by search engines and social media, have created an infrastructure of advertising, bidding, and matching at a scale that makes finding a match between an advertising message and a potential customer more likely. There also exists the potential for the value created by advertising to be shared more widely, as Google does with their publishing partners in their AdSense, or YouTube does with their video providers. Even in these cases, the digital company controlling the advertising network will take 30% of the revenue for simply making a successful match. Transaction-based models, where buyers and sellers can be matched for a fee or a percentage of a transaction, could distribute wealth more widely if a new group of sellers is created, such as the hosts on Airbnb who would have never otherwise rented out a room. The company running the platform, however, still has the best opportunity to capture value, and to experiment with different value-sharing methods that might optimize their own revenue.

For almost every business model in the digital world, there is the potential for wealth concentration, but this is not a theoretical necessity. Shifts in wealth distribution will ultimately depend on the business models chosen by digital technology companies, and the mediation and mobilization choices they make to implement those models. To answer the larger question about technology and inequality, we will need to examine the practices used by these companies to see exactly where value is created, where it is captured, and if there are viable alternatives.

NOTES

1. See Orlikowski (2000) for the academic roots of the 'practice lens' idea.
2. See Ries (2011) and Blank (2013).
3. My favorite example being YouTube starting as a dating service.
4. Verbeek uses the example of fetal ultrasound, which creates a new moral choice about whether to proceed with the birth of a fetus with known genetic defects.
5. See Keizer (2014), though lower profit margins can also be a deliberate strategy of one side subsidizing the other, rather than an inherent difference in software versus hardware profitability.

References

Akrich, M. (1992). The de-scription of technical objects. In W. E. Bijker & J. Law (Eds.), *Shaping technology/building society: Studies in sociotechnical change* (pp. 205–224). Cambridge, MA: MIT Press.

Bijker, W. E., Hughes, T. P., & Pinch, T. J. (Eds.). (1987). *The social construction of technological systems: New directions in the sociology and history of technology.* Cambridge, MA: MIT Press.

Blank, S. (2013). Why the lean start-up changes everything. *Harvard Business Review, 91*(5), 63–72.

Courage, C., & Baxter, K. (2005). *Understanding your users: A practical guide to user requirements methods, tools, and techniques.* San Francisco, CA: Gulf Professional Publishing.

Elliott, M. S., & Kraemer, K. L. (Eds.). (2008). *Computerization movements and technology diffusion: From mainframes to ubiquitous computing.* Medford, NJ: Information Today Inc.

Gilbert, R. J. (2015). E-books: A tale of digital disruption. *The Journal of Economic Perspectives, 29*(3), 165–184.

Keizer, G. (2014). Microsoft's quandary: Big profits from software or shrinking margins with devices. Retrieved February 22, 2017, from http://www.computerworld.com/article/2486968/it-management/microsoft-s-quandary–big-profits-from-software-or-shrinking-margins–with-devices.html.

Laing, A., & Royle, J. (2013). Bookselling online: An examination of consumer behaviour patterns. *Publishing Research Quarterly, 29*(2), 110–127.

Latour, B. (2005). *Reassembling the social: An introduction to actor-network-theory.* New York: Oxford University Press.

Linden, G., Kraemer, K. L., & Dedrick, J. (2009). Who captures value in a global innovation network? The case of Apple's iPod. *Communications of the ACM, 52*(3), 140–144.

MacKenzie, D., & Spinardi, G. (1995). Tacit knowledge, weapons design, and the uninvention of nuclear weapons. *American Journal of Sociology, 101*(1), 44–99.

Myers, G. J., Sandler, C., & Badgett, T. (2011). *The art of software testing* (3rd ed.). Hoboken, NJ: Wiley.

Orlikowski, W. J. (2000). Using technology and constituting structures: A practice lens for studying technology in organizations. *Organization Science, 11*(4), 404–428.

Osterwalder, A., & Pigneur, Y. (2010). *Business model generation: A handbook for visionaries, game changers, and challengers.* Hoboken, NJ: Wiley.

Ries, E. (2011). *The lean startup: How today's entrepreneurs use continuous innovation to create radically successful businesses.* New York: Crown Business.

Russo, N., Kehl, D., Morgus, R., & Morris, S. (2014). The cost of connectivity 2014. Retrieved February 2, 2017, from https://www.newamerica.org/oti/policy-papers/the-cost-of-connectivity-2014/.

Seufert, E. B. (2013). *Freemium economics: Leveraging analytics and user segmentation to drive revenue*. Waltham, MA: Morgan Kaufmann.

Teece, D. J. (2010). Business models, business strategy and innovation. *Long Range Planning, 43*(2), 172–194.

Verbeek, P.-P. (2006). Materializing morality: Design ethics and technological mediation. *Science, Technology and Human Values, 31*(3), 361–380.

Verbeek, P.-P. (2015). Beyond interaction: A short introduction to mediation theory. *Interactions, 22*(3), 26–31.

CHAPTER 6

Technology and Inequality Case Study: Search

Abstract Using our simple conceptual framework of mediation, model, mobilization, and wealth effects, we analyze the case of online search. Search is a high-stakes commercial activity that strongly influences consumer attention and action. The mediation of search is an evolving contest between search companies trying to provide results that serve their business model needs, and expand their reach, while other players attempt to understand the secretive algorithms behind search engines for their own promotion purposes. The business model of search, tied to advertising auctions, has been highly profitable, and resulted in a highly concentrated search industry.

Keywords Google · Search engines · Electronic commerce · Secretive algorithms · Business models

6.1 Digital Mediation of Search

Studying digital mediation means analyzing the choices made about digital representations. These representations mediate two different types of relationships: between humans and the world, and between humans and each other. The representation choices affect human action and perception. By describing the choices made, an analysis of mediation also highlights the choices not made. An analysis of digital mediation seeks to answer two questions: what were the specific mediation choices made? And what difference did those choices make?

For search engines, the most basic digital mediation is between people searching for information and the information available on the world wide web. The web is the largest universe of information in history, with its hundreds of millions of domain names and trillions of individual pages. The most basic representational choice involves how one chooses—from among billions of possibilities—a small set of results in response to a request for information.

Which results come first, and how they are shown, is one of the most extreme manifestations of the power of representation, and one that happens to have serious commercial consequences. The top search results are much more likely to be seen and acted upon. Very few searchers look beyond the first page of results, and people tend to trust higher ranked results, even if their actual relevance is not as high (Pan et al. 2007). The influence of this mediation is strong, and while the act of searching makes the influence of the representation apparent, our willingness to trust its results gives the influence of this technology a hidden aspect as well.

As discussed in Chap. 3, online product searches have become one of the most common ways consumers find products and services, particularly from local businesses. The representation of search results changes perceptions of the world, amplifying the selected content while reducing others. Perception changes become action changes when customers are either invited to visit a business with a click-through, or inhibited from visiting. For the search engine company, one of the most important representational choices is whether content providers can pay for a better search result. A second, related choice is how the search engine provider will rank their own products and services.

The history of search contains a variety of mediation options. One possibility is human curation, as in the original Yahoo! Internet directory, and in the portal business model of AOL popular in the first dot. com era of the late 1990s. Another possibility is to use information retrieval techniques to analyze the content of web pages, as was used by Google's earliest competition, DEC's AltaVista engine. An approach that emerged later was to use the recommendations of friends or like-minded individuals, as seen in social media or collaborative news-filtering sites. Thrown into this mix are different techniques for paid placement and sponsored results.

Google's search engine used what was then a new mediation choice: the link structure of the entire world wide web. With access to unique resources, including a significant fraction of Stanford University's networking and computing capacity at the time,[1] Google's founders were able to experiment with, and prove the value of, this representation. Google used the structure of the web itself—the hyperlinks between pages—as a community assessment of the quality of content. Pages with many links pointing to them had a higher reputation; and a link from a page with high reputation would increase reputation as well. This reputational ranking was combined with a growing set of additional variables about web pages and their context into the proprietary Google algorithm.

The other representational choice Google made was to separate search results into 'organic' and 'paid.' This separation maintained trust in the regular, organic results, which were produced by a secret algorithm weighing over 200 different factors. The exact list of factors, and their respective weights, was never revealed. Even paid results rankings were not complete determined by which advertiser bid the most, but also considered how relevant the results were for consumers. Paid results that earned more consumer clicks would move up in the rankings, even if an advertiser bid a lower price per click. This quality check meant even the paid results were perceived as more relevant and trustworthy, and less intrusive than the representations used at competitor sites.

In terms of preferential treatment for their own content and services, this has been a point of contention between Google and regulators (European Commission 2016). As part of its mission to provide access to all information, as well as feed their business model with ever growing streams of traffic, Google has developed and acquired a massive set of online services on their own for mapping, shopping, email, news, videos, analytics, language translation, and social media, with some being more successful than others. The temptation to promote their own services, especially when they are less successful, will remain, but, because of the lack of transparency in the search algorithm, it is difficult to know the extent of this behavior, short of legal and regulatory proceedings.

Over time, this lack of transparency in search representations created a kind of arms race with other content and service providers. Content providers have learned how to improve their search results through the dark arts of search engine optimization (Malaga 2008), engaging in a continual effort to reverse engineer the secret Google algorithms.

Google, in turn, keeps their methods secret to thwart these attempts to, in their view, 'game the system,' causing regular changes to their already complex algorithm.

Early in the search engine ranking game, content providers, seeking to improve their search results, could create links to the site they wanted to promote, or pay others with high reputations to link to their site. Google responded by discounting links from relatively new sites or sites of low reputation. More recently, some publishers have copied and assembled content from other web sites, occasionally earning higher search engine rankings than the original authors. Google's algorithm now downgrades any site it believes is copying rather than creating new content. Search placement has become a running battle, a continuously evolving contest between the platform provider and those who wish to increase their visibility on the platform. The lifeblood of online businesses, acquiring customers, depends on the results.

How search is mediated becomes a key issue for the individual consumer when privacy is taken into account. Search histories are filled with extremely detailed, highly sensitive information that can affect employment, reputation, legal proceedings,[2] and personal relationships. Google has chosen for the most part to keep this data for their own purposes, to better improve their own business model, even though search data in the aggregate has potential predictive value for economic indicators and decisions, especially purchase decisions (Choi and Varian 2012). So far, Google has been able to avoid serious regulatory restrictions on stockpiling this unprecedented level of personally identifiable information.

6.2 The Search Business Model

The search business model, as implemented by Google, is advertising. Almost 90% of Google's annual revenue, which is now approaching $100 billion US dollars, comes from advertising. Eighty percent of advertising revenue comes from advertisements on Google's own web sites and services, such as the paid results displayed next to organic search results, and video advertisements on YouTube. The other 20% of advertising revenue comes from advertisements placed on other publisher's sites.

A business model describes both value creation and value capture. In terms of value creation, Google's search engine when it was first launched was a clearly superior product for finding web information.[3]

Consumer use has shown its value for purchasing decisions. The next challenge was value capture. How would a search engine make money? Most of the infamous dot.com companies of the late 1990s struggled to find a way of converting huge online audiences into profits, and never succeeded at finding an answer. Google began as a company without a clear idea of how to make money, and its first business models were to license its technology to other companies, and to sell hardware boxes for internal searches in large corporate data centers.

Then, through a series of experiments and encounters, Google found the advertising business model that had eluded so many other startups. The model was difficult to find because it required the unique combination of at least four different elements: relevant paid search results separated from regular results; self-service advertisement design and purchase; a bidding auction for paid search placement; and payments based on customer clicks rather than advertising views. The previous section mentioned the importance of separating paid results from organic ones, and moving the more effective paid advertisements higher in their rankings for consumer usefulness. The ability of advertisers to self-create a simple advertisement online and ask for payment via a credit card meant they were no longer forced to work through an expensive and slow sales process. Advertisers bid for better placements, with Google using a classic auction design of the winner only being charged the price of the second-place bid to ensure no auction winners would be punished for bidding too highly. And, unlike the standard industry practice of charging for advertisements based on number of views, Google advertisers would only pay if customers clicked on an advertisement and went to their site. Paying per click allowed advertisers to precisely track which advertisements worked, making it much easier to determine return on investment than merely displaying messages. All four of these elements came together to create Google AdWords, the service that Levy called the greatest money-making machine in the history of the Internet. According to Levy, when Google was finally forced to reveal how profitable they were in their 2004 Initial Public Offering, investors were shocked.

Most of Google's major acquisitions over the next decade can be seen as extending their search business model by bringing more customers to Google advertisements. For example, Google acquired the technology for AdSense, allowing them to publish relevant advertisements on other sites, based on an automatic assessment of that site's content.

When Google acquired what became Google Analytics, they gave it away for free, allowing advertisers to better track the value of their Google advertising investments, and experiment with improving them; but when Google acquired the technology for Google Docs, and developed Gmail to bring in more visitors, they had a difficult time convincing people that advertisements based on the content of personal emails were legitimate. They then acquired YouTube for a high price at the time, $1.6 billion US, to replace their own unsuccessful Google Video service. They later acquired DoubleClick to expand their ability to serve advertising more widely and to improve their real-time auction capabilities. Perhaps most importantly, Google acquired and then developed the Android mobile operating system to ensure that visitors from mobile devices would continue to use Google services, knowing Android and the Chrome web browser were their best guarantees that the billions of visits required for their business model to thrive would continue into the future. Intelligent assistants may be the next piece of technology in the struggle to maintain access to customers.

With their superior early product, and a new advertising model that removed irrelevant and distracting display ads, Google had no trouble convincing users of the customer value proposition, especially because it was free to use. But keeping the business model together required a number of other challenging relationships and resources. The world wide web had to continue as a useful source of information to be mined, and it had to continue to grow on its own. Those parties trying to manipulate the web through search engine optimization created more than some difficulty.

The search business model would need to keep the participation of both advertisers, and advertisement publishers. Google would also need the assistance of Internet partners such as Yahoo! and AOL for visitor traffic, especially early on. Google would need to attract sophisticated computer science and business talent in order to solve their unprecedented challenges of technological scale. Fortunately for Google, the unique advertising model they eventually perfected generated so much profit they had the financial resources to meet the challenges of implementing their highly complex business model.

Perhaps equally important was the value that Google decided not to capture. In the course of their searches, Google's customers leave a detailed record of what they are looking for, and whether they have successfully found it, data that could have been packaged and sold for marketing purposes. Instead, Google used this data internally, as a means to improve their own search technology. With a larger stream of visitors, and unprecedented visibility into their actions, Google was able to relentlessly experiment on their own users, and use the results of what would come to be known as 'A/B testing' to improve their search results. Finding a valuable use for this unique data without upsetting customers was another victory for the new search business model.

6.3 Mobilizing for Search

The grand vision of search engine providers like Google was to make all the world's information available to augment human intelligence. Once all the world's information was collected and organized, artificial intelligence and machine learning technologies would make humans smarter by providing knowledge instantly and everywhere (Stross 2008). This vision was broad enough to attract some of the world's best computer science and business talent while at the same time not demanding any sacrifices from other parties, such as consumers, advertisers, and publishers, who came to search engines for more pragmatic reasons. The vision was grandiose enough to attract the most prestigious venture capital investors of the day. The main resistance to the grand vision would come from foreign governments, and from existing industries such as booksellers, who were unenthused about making their information assets available for free.

In terms of generic parties to be mobilized for the search business model to succeed over time, we can identify at least five: advertisers, advertisement publishers, advertising consumers, the world wide web, and regulators. Investors are usually an influential group for technology startups. However, because of the founder's university connections, their early prototyping success, and their relatively early discovery of a successful way to capture value, Google faced few challenges from investors. Early angel and venture capital investors wanting to invest in Google were in abundance. High profitability and healthy cash flow gave Google the freedom to maneuver. Even the purchase of YouTube, and a few years of operating their video service at a loss, was all handled without outside financing.

Advertisers and advertisement publishers are the two main parties brought together by a search engine company, matching buyers and sellers. Advertisers are kept on board through ease of use, and a stream of profitable customers who respond to their advertisements by clicking through to their sites. The AdWords service provided ease of use and self-service, while Google Analytics allowed advertisers to track the results of their investments with precision. Without this detailed information, advertisers might defect to social media or other platforms that offered more customer exposure.

Advertisement publishers are kept on board the search business model with a healthy stream of revenue payments, and ease of use. With the AdSense service, Google has become the advertising network of choice for small publishers. AdSense automatically chooses the advertising that best matches publisher content from Google's large advertisement inventory, without the publisher having to do more than sign up and paste a bit of code onto their sites.

Both parties derive more value from the site because of the depth of Google's massive advertising network. The larger the inventory of advertisements and publishers, the more effectively the platform can link the two for any customer. Advertisers pay for clicks, and sometimes views, while publishers receive a percentage of the advertising revenue, typically around 70%. Advertisers need to be able to calculate their customer acquisition costs precisely and compare those to the profitability of new customers. The conversion rate, or the percentage of potential customers who take a desired action that leads to business value, becomes critical for keeping advertisers on board. Bringing the two sides together creates major size benefits, chief among them having the largest advertising network inventory. More precise targeting is immediately rewarded with higher conversion rates and more valuable online actions, making advertising networks similar in their winner-take-all dynamic to other forms of digital technology.

Google provides web analytic technology which allows advertisers to precisely monitor how their advertising expenditures lead to online actions. By providing sophisticated web tracking technology for free, Google increases the value of their main AdWords service. Google has become the dominant provider of web analytics services in the US as a result, giving them even further insight into online customer behavior. Google has been able to increase its overall advertising revenue consistently—even as the value of individual ad clicks has decreased—by increasing the scope of searches that can be advertised against.

For the business model to work, large volumes of customers have to be consistently mobilized to participate. If customers stop visiting, stop paying attention to advertisements, or stop taking online action, the model will not hold together. Even with conversion rates of around 1–2%, the business model can produce consistent financial results due to traffic volumes in millions, or even billions.

The search model requires that customer actions be tracked in minute detail. If customers refuse to be tracked, the model ceases to work. For the analytics technology to work best, customers must have certain technologies enabled in their devices or browsers, such as the javascript code that reports customer behaviors back to Google's servers, and browser cookies that uniquely identify individuals. Customers have yet to rebel against this detailed kind of tracking. Despite the theoretical risks of personalized data tracking, it is difficult to find examples of individual harm due to consumer search histories.

Customers continue to participate in the business model with the expectation that search results return valuable information. This means that the health of the world wide web is a key issue for the search model. Without relevant information being published and updated on the web, customers will look elsewhere. With the exception of traditional news outlets and book publishers, Google has faced little resistance from the web. The more significant challenges are from other major technology platforms, such as Facebook and Amazon, that do not make most of their information available on the web, and therefore visible to Google.

Regulators are an important stakeholder whose cooperation must be maintained. In the US, federal trade regulations govern online advertising, but few new regulations have been created for online advertising specifically, and new privacy regulations limiting the tracking of individual behavior online have been minimal. The European Union requires individually identifiable data to be tracked, and affords customers certain rights to inspect information about themselves. Consumer regulations in the US are less stringent. Information cannot be sold to third parties in some cases, but there are few restrictions on how the information can be combined with other databases.

The most serious regulatory moves against Google's business model have come from only the largest government institutions. The European Union has brought multiple anti-trust cases against Google, and Google recently withdrew from China, unable to repair their complex relationship with the Chinese government. In these few but significant cases, Google has not been able to maintain their business model in the face of large-scale political pressure. Otherwise, their business model has successfully mobilized all the required parties, and continues to do so.

6.4 The Wealth Effects of Search

But how, exactly, has the search business model affected the distribution of wealth? To begin, we know the search business is highly concentrated. In the US, Google's market share of online searches is close to 80% and growing, especially on mobile devices (Southern 2016), and in the European Union it is even higher, at nearly 90% of searches (Scott 2016). Only similar large technology companies, like Microsoft, are able to compete with this market dominance. In China, the leading search engine Baidu handles nearly 80% of Internet searches, and a similar share of search advertising revenues. The leading Russian search engine, Yandex, handles over 50% of online searches in their home country, but faces increasing competition from Google (Symington 2016). All of the leading search companies follow Google's advertisement-based business model, use similar forms of technological mediation, and have to mobilize the same types of actors for the model to function.

Industry concentration has led to significant wealth creation. Google's parent company, Alphabet, has created half a trillion dollars US in market capitalization, and generates almost $100 billion in revenue annually while employing only around 75,000 people, 20,000 of whom are in research and development (Alphabet 2016). The tiered voting structure of Alphabet 'B' shares allows a small group of founders and early employees to control decision-making over this wealth.

In terms of wages and compensation, Google's pay is high for managers and engineers. Like many other technology companies, compensation through equity shares and options in addition to regular wages runs into the billions of dollars a year. For non-technical work, debate exists over whether these highly profitable technology companies give higher pay or benefits, or are just as likely to use subcontractors and part-time temporary workers at much lower wages as other companies.[4]

Even with wealth concentration through equity ownership and compensation, it is possible that wealth becomes less concentrated for other stakeholders in the business model. Google pays out a significant fraction of its revenues as traffic acquisition costs, which could be more widely distributed, as in the case of small publishers. Small businesses and individuals selling online could be benefitting broadly from the search business model, but the benefits would have to be on a scale comparable to the wealth directly created and concentrated by the search business model.

In general, there is little evidence that electronic commerce sales are becoming less concentrated in the US, despite early predictions of a more level playing field. Major technology platforms such as Amazon are taking a growing percentage of electronic commerce retail revenue. Digital technology's influence over purchasing decisions has not yet led to an increase in new companies in the US, or an overall reduction in company size, though we lack the studies to test these theories directly.

For consumers, there are logical reasons why search might increase their overall welfare through better information and potentially lower prices. Google publishes its own estimates of consumer benefits on the order of tens of billions of US dollars, but these would need to be compared to other independent assessments of consumer benefits.[5] As online commerce is still only 10–15% of US retail sales, these consumer benefits might not be big enough yet to affect larger trends in wealth inequality.

For the world wide web community as a whole, there are widespread benefits to having a viable business model that supports a free and open information sharing platform, and a healthy world wide web could lead to more business opportunity. Thriving communities for open software and standards, along with neutral treatment of Internet traffic, open the possibility of new technology startups emerging.

For governments and their regulators, online commerce in general has been subject to lower taxation. In the US, tax is not automatically collected for transactions that cross state borders, giving online vendors significant practical advantages over their local competition. Perhaps not surprisingly, Google itself is one of the largest users of international tax avoidance strategies.

The end result of the search business model is the creation of a highly profitable, highly concentrated new industry, with a company at its center that is able to use its resources to satisfy its stakeholders, resist pressures from investors, and acquire new competitors as they arise. The company at the center of the model has the ability to experiment on its customers and partners, exclusively own a uniquely powerful database of consumer behavior, and has the capacity to scale to global size. All of these basic advantages provide numerous opportunities to optimize value capture from the model, with the wealth from that value capture accruing to a relatively concentrated set of people.

Though clearly more evidence is needed to precisely quantify the wealth effects for many of the stakeholders in the search business model, we see few dramatic signs of decreasing wealth concentration through search, either directly in online commerce, or indirectly through small business and individuals generally. This particular form of technological mediation requires highly detailed tracking of individual behavior, which is linked to advertising. The unique database of customer activities is difficult for others to replicate. The model is so profitable that the company controlling it can use their large cash reserves, and highly valued equity shares, to acquire any new companies that would broaden the scope of their business model, or potentially compete against it. The advertising business model offers small players and individuals the possibility of competing with larger companies, or the targeting of new niches, but there are powerful concentration effects from having the largest advertising network, with larger inventories of advertisements and publishers making advertising more effective and profitable.

So, the question becomes: Can the search business model be changed to reduce any wealth-concentrating effects? We can look to each element of our simple framework for possible answers. To shift the business model of search away from advertising would be to walk away from one of the most successful value capture schemes in digital history, so the benefits of changing would have to be equally large. In terms of mediation, the most likely possibility is to imagine a different interface for finding products and services. Because search engines are facing direct competition from social media and online shopping platforms, these technology alternatives, or some new combination of them, could provide a different mix of perception and action changes that might be more broadening than the extreme focus of search engine results.

Mobilization strategies are another potential source of change. The entire business model depends on cooperation from consumers and openly providing information on the web. Changes could begin if consumers perceive search as less effective, rebel against the collection of personally identifiable information, or organize some kind of boycott due to outside events. Consumer defections have yet to occur on any meaningful scale, but remain a theoretical possibility if a mass movement can be created. Web publishers could block search engines from accessing their content, but there have been few signs of rebellion here either. The obvious alternatives to the search model—social media giants such as Facebook, and online commerce giants such as Amazon—appear equally likely to concentrate wealth, and for similar reasons.

Notes

1. See Levy (2011) for this story and many other details of the early history of Google.
2. See Carr (2008) for examples of how even anonymized individual search data can be revealing, and sometimes traceable back to a person.
3. Levy (2011) describes how impressed early users of Google were versus the competition.
4. See Sydell (2013) for an account of part-time security work, (O'Brien 2015) for wages and unionization issues with technology company bus drivers.
5. See Ratchford et al. (2003) for examples of how to compute potential the potential consumer benefits of internet searches. Estimates for individual markets can be as high as hundreds of millions of US. The distribution of benefits usually is not calculated, but presumably in consumer markets the benefits would be highly distributed.

References

Alphabet. (2016). Alphabet investor relations. Retrieved February 4, 2017, from https://abc.xyz/investor/.

Carr, N. G. (2008). *The big switch: Rewiring the world, from Edison to Google*. New York: W. W. Norton.

Choi, H., & Varian, H. (2012). Predicting the present with Google Trends. *Economic Record*, 88(s1), 2–9.

European Commission. (2016). Antitrust: Commission takes further steps in investigations alleging Google's comparison shopping and advertising-related practices breach EU rules. Retrieved February 4, 2017, from http://europa.eu/rapid/press-release_IP-16-2532_en.htm.

Levy, S. (2011). *In the plex: How Google thinks, works, and shapes our lives*. New York: Simon and Schuster.

Malaga, R. A. (2008). Worst practices in search engine optimization. *Communications of the ACM*, 51(12), 147–150.

O'Brien, M. (2015). Google shuttle drivers to see pay hike, better benefits. Retrieved February 5, 2017, from http://www.mercurynews.com/2015/03/11/google-shuttle-drivers-to-see-pay-hike-better-benefits/.

Pan, B., Hembrooke, H., Joachims, T., Lorigo, L., Gay, G., & Granka, L. (2007). In Google we trust: Users' decisions on rank, position, and relevance. *Journal of Computer-Mediated Communication*, 12(3), 801–823.

Ratchford, B. T., Pan, X., & Shankar, V. (2003). On the efficiency of internet markets for consumer goods. *Journal of Public Policy & Marketing*, 22(1), 4–16.

Scott, M. (2016). Google rebuts antitrust claims in Europe. Retrieved February 5, 2017, from https://www.nytimes.com/2016/11/04/technology/google-eu-antitrust-europe.html.
Southern, M. (2016). Latest search market share numbers: Google search up across all devices. Retrieved February 5, 2017, from https://www.searchenginejournal.com/august-2016-search-market-share/172078/.
Stross, R. (2008). *Planet Google: One company's audacious plan to organize everything we know.* New York: Simon & Schuster.
Sydell, L. (2013). What it's like to live on low pay in a land of plenty. Retrieved February 5, 2017, from http://www.npr.org/sections/alltechconsidered/2013/12/17/251992536/security-guards-at-big-tech-companies-struggle-with-low-pay.
Symington, S. (2016). Yandex gains after a strong quarter despite losing market share. Retrieved February 5, 2017, from https://www.fool.com/investing/2016/10/29/yandex-gains-after-a-strong-quarter-despite-losing.aspx.

CHAPTER 7

Technology and Inequality Case Study: Social Media

Abstract Using our four-part framework of mediation, model, mobilization, and wealth effects, this chapter analyzes social media as a case study of technology and inequality. The digital mediation of social relationships has evolved from personal profiles and networks of friends and followers to an information feed that keeps users updated about new content in their social network. The attractiveness of social media as an online activity is unprecedented. Like the search industry, social media has found a lucrative advertising-based business model that requires careful decisions about how commercial messages are injected into people's social news streams. Social media information feeds are now controlled by proprietary algorithms that try to highlight enticing and commercially relevant content, making the resulting social media industry highly concentrated (though not as concentrated as search) and highly profitable.

Keywords Social media · Facebook · Business models · News feeds

7.1 Digital Mediation of Social Media

Social media represents human relationships digitally. The original form of representation was the personal profile. Individuals would present information about themselves—often surprisingly detailed information—and others would visit these profiles. Even with this basic functionality, checking other people's profiles was surprisingly engaging. For example, it was not uncommon for early Facebook users to look at dozens, if not hundreds, of profiles per day.[1] By revealing key pieces of information about members, such as their photos and relationship statuses, social media sites spread rapidly, often faster than the technology infrastructure could handle.

The other important form of representation was the social network. Individuals would 'friend' each other, forming a network of social relationships. Friends lists became a new form of self-expression, but were also useful for meeting new people through friends-of-friends, and for determining how profile information was shared. Other features were added to social media that took advantage of detailed profile and social network information. The sharing of photos, events, and online discussions, for instance, became more engaging when automatically tied to people's existing social networks.

The most important change in how human relationships were represented was the transition from profiles to news feeds. Instead of manually scanning profiles to see new comments or 'likes,' Facebook's founders believed people wanted to see all their social network updates in one place. The news feed shifted digital mediation from a person-to-person network, toward a stream of information about the larger world. The news feed would eventually include updates from businesses, news media, and groups and organizations of all kinds.

According to Kirkpatrick, the overhaul of Facebook's site to represent news feeds was the most complex product development in their history to date, and the most controversial. Early users complained that news feeds, by broadcasting so many social interactions at such a detailed level, felt like digital 'stalking.' The news feed is now the default representation used to mediate social networks. When news feeds were first launched, it quickly became apparent that content could propagate through social networks much more rapidly, and on a much larger scale, than with the previous mediation based on profiles, ushering in the birth of 'virality.'

The news feed began as a list of updates, newest first, from friends and likes. As the volume of traffic grew, Facebook provided two different news feeds: one feed with every update from the social network; and one feed with the most relevant items selected by Facebook's algorithm. Social media sites such as LinkedIn learned from examining their own data that the most recent updates were not always the most interesting (Agarwal et al. 2014), or most likely to result in a further action on site. Facebook's algorithm weighed factors such as whether a person had interacted with (i.e., commented on or liked) similar content before, or had interacted with a person or group recently. Just as with search, however, the exact workings of the news feed algorithm were kept secret (Bucher 2012). The social media companies learned from their detailed user data how to improve their algorithms, increasing the likelihood people would return to the site and interact with news feed items.

Two further representation choices were fundamental for social media. The first decision was whether to allow anonymity or require people to use their real-world identities. Prior to Facebook and Friendster, its most similar predecessor, discussion boards and multiuser games used account names rather than real names. Research on these anonymous (or pseudonymous) online environments focused on how people used online social interactions to explore new identities.

Facebook, in contrast, demanded a real identity, at first tied to a real university email address. Using real names not only matched with the existing practice of printed 'facebooks' at private US universities, but also reflected the values of their main founder and his belief in the societal benefits of 'radical transparency.' Academic research on Facebook began to investigate whether social media profiles reflected a person's true personality, or were more about people portraying themselves as they wished to be seen by others. Early research suggested that when using real identities, college students used social media to appear 'popular,' 'well-rounded,' and 'thoughtful' online (Zhao et al. 2008). Students achieved this self-presentation less by describing themselves in an elaborate profile and more by showing their personality through behaviors such as comments and likes.

Later research argued that social media with real names made it difficult for online behavior to reflect anything other than a person's real personality (Back et al. 2010). Information on social media was too difficult to control, and friends were able to provide feedback on any online behaviors, such as bragging, that might appear to be inauthentic. Early research also found correlations between aspects of personality and social media use. High narcissism and low self-esteem were associated with more Facebook activity (Mehdizadeh 2010), supporting the argument that social media reflected true personality. Different types of people used social media differently, with extroverts updating more frequently, people with higher self-esteem posting less frequently about romantic partners, and narcissists saying more about their own achievements (Marshall et al. 2015).

Using an anonymous representation for social media had some advantages. It was easier to meet new people on Facebook's competitor, MySpace, that did not require real identities (Dwyer et al. 2007), where there was more freedom on profiles to express identity by modifying code and graphics on profile pages. Facebook's use of real identities led to it being used more for maintaining pre-existing relationships rather than starting new ones (Pempek et al. 2009), a major benefit of Facebook, especially for more casual relationships with fewer interactions. More Facebook use was correlated with higher amounts of social capital (Ellison et al. 2007), or stronger real-world relationships, and Facebook was also able to overcome the obvious privacy objections involved in sharing detailed personal information online. The Facebook community, at first limited to only college students, felt safe, even as it was opened to the outside world in part because early users believed their personal information was being shared only with people like themselves (Acquisti and Gross 2006).

Social media use with real identities grew so rapidly that the reasons for their powerful lure, and their effects on individuals, became major research topics. In contrast to earlier studies, research began to emphasize the decreases in happiness associated with higher social media use (Sagioglou and Greitemeyer 2014). Too much social media use resulted in a feeling of wasted time, and depressive symptoms tended to increase as people compared their own lives with others, or at least other people's online representations.[2] As news feeds incorporated more images, users on newer sites like Instagram continued to use social media for 'surveillance' of their friends' lives, and 'documentation' of their own (Sheldon and Bryant 2016).

A second fundamental representation choice was how to incorporate commercial messages. Paid advertisements could be displayed on a user's home page or profile, but could they also be included in groups, events, or even in the news feed itself? Once social media sites transitioned to a news feed representation, commercial messages could be incorporated in the results generated by a proprietary algorithm, in essence buying their way to higher feed placement, but always with an uncertain weighting. This launched a similar dynamic to search engine optimization, with experts trying to reverse engineer the algorithms and appear higher in the feed results (Bucher 2012). When commercial messages were combined with friend behavior (for example, a message saying your friend just bought 'x') in the Facebook Beacon experiment, that proved a step too far, even for Facebook's users (Kirkpatrick 2011).

At first, there were two news feeds, one unfiltered and one chosen by the platform. Over time, the unfiltered feed disappeared. Commercial interests would only be able to reach audiences through the workings of the news feed algorithm, only reaching people who asked to follow a business or product. Businesses that went to the effort of building a list of potential customers through their Facebook pages were no longer guaranteed their messages would be seen. Since algorithmic control arrived, there have been controversies about how news feed results are determined, among them: too many commercial messages, and too many updates from people who are not real friends. People's own behavior reinforces what they wish to see in the news feed, potentially reducing the diversity of the messages they receive (Bakshy et al. 2015).

7.2 The Social Media Business Model

The social media business, interestingly, began without a business model. Revenue was a lower priority than building a critical mass of users. Using low-cost, highly scalable technology reduced the pressure to earn revenue in the early stages. According to Kirkpatrick, Facebook began on servers costing $85 US dollars per month (and would cost only a few dollars today). Even after their first summer, with over 200,000 users, Facebook's founders had only spent $85 thousand US dollars. Given their higher income background, Facebook's founders were easily able to raise money themselves. Once social media had proven itself with actual users, raising subsequent money from investors was relatively easy. Facebook achieved explosive growth in their initial student markets, and this growth would have been unlikely if those early customers were charged a fee to use the service.

Like search, advertising has become the main business model for social media. Compared to search, social media offers advantages for the advertising model. Social media attracts much more consumer time than any other online platform, with 55% of Facebook users in the US visiting several times per day (Greenwood et al. 2016). Social media users tend to share more profile information than other types of online activity, so advertisers are able to target specific demographics and interest groups. This is particularly useful for brand awareness advertising, which earns money for displaying messages, as opposed to a cost-per-click model typically used in search.

The advertising business model has become highly profitable for social media. At Facebook, the largest social media company, the fraction of revenue coming from advertising has actually increased over time, to over 97% in 2016 (Facebook 2017), with a mere 17,000 Facebook employees generating almost $28 billion US in revenues, and $10 billion profit, in 2016. Despite this, the Facebook business model faced a technological challenge as their users switched from desktop computers to mobile devices. The ability of the advertising business model to work for mobile devices was unproven, and brought new limitations, such as screen size. Such is the attractiveness of social media, however, that users stayed on board, with more than 80% of Facebook's advertising revenue now coming from mobile devices, suggesting their experiments with new forms of mobile advertising delivery have proved successful so far.

As the mediation of social media moved from profiles toward more of a continuous news feed, new challenges and opportunities appeared for the advertising business model. Using its earlier profiles, Facebook was able to charge for display advertising. The first attempts at targeting were advertising 'flyers' for students at a particular university, promoting sponsored business pages and discussion groups. The shift to a news feed offered the opportunity for commercial messaging to enter the flow of information from friends and family. The social media platforms then needed to experiment with what kind of commercial messages could appear in the news feed without upsetting users, as well as how often. Thus far, more commercial messaging in the news feed has yet to lead to any kind of serious user revolt, or even many complaints, despite some concern about increased clutter in news feeds. Should the need arise, social media companies are uniquely equipped to address any concerns, as they can experiment with the placement and frequency of commercial messages to see their exact effects on usage and engagement.

As the news feed transitioned to algorithmic control, advertisers were offered the ability to promote messages in news feeds, increasing their visibility. Businesses that had built their customer lists online through social media, with the expectation of being able to contact them as they pleased, were now often required to pay Facebook in order to reach their own customers. As this practice gains in acceptance, paying to promote messages in news feeds has become a valuable source of income for Facebook. The social media platform truly serves as an intermediary between businesses and customers, which, in terms of value capture through an advertising model, is exactly the right place to be.

Some opportunities have opened for social media specialists, along the lines of search engine optimization specialists, who are able to master the complexities of the ever-changing secret algorithms in order to get commercial messages across more effectively. Because the news feed algorithm evaluates the amount of user interaction with content, this provides opportunities for commercial entities, perhaps new ones, to play the attention game more effectively than established large firms.

At a key stage in their history, Facebook faced a choice of either charging users, selling data, or charging advertisers (Marichal 2016). Charging advertisers has become a key part of their highly successful business model, but other strategies were tried along the way. Facebook hoped, at one point, that payments and digital purchases would become a valuable revenue source. Social media platforms were opened to third party software developers, making 'in app' purchasing a potential business model, but experience showed that social media apps tended to focus on gaming and other lightweight entertainment that had limited payment value. This business model remains a tiny niche. There were also experiments with retail electronic commerce directly on social media sites, under the theory that consumers would be happy to buy where they spend so much of their time already, though direct purchasing on social media has been a shrinking business model so far. And, like search, the social media companies have kept their highly valuable user information to themselves rather than selling it to others.

7.3 Mobilizing for Social Media

The most critical people to be mobilized in the early phases of social media were the end users, mostly students, for whom social media provided an exciting new capability at seemingly no cost beyond their (presumably abundant) leisure time and their willingness to disclose information about themselves.

But social media knew it faced a problem of acquiring critical mass—why would anyone use social media if their friends and family were not already there? Understanding that a critical mass of interaction was required for a community-based system, Facebook's platform was released in phases—first, a single university, then similar universities, then other types of schools—before finally being opened to the general public. Online review platforms such as Yelp used a similar strategy, building a critical mass of reviews in few cities before rolling out to other areas. Beyond critical mass, a phased rollout also provided an 'imagined community' of people like themselves (Acquisti and Gross 2006), a place where it was much more comfortable to share personal information during a time when Facebook was perceived as 'only for students.'

Early social media platforms experimented with new forms of interaction that would keep online users coming back more often. Some social media platforms, such as MySpace, gave users more technical control over their own profile pages, enticing them to create ever more elaborate profiles. Other platforms offered more fine-grained control over how updates would be shared. Facebook kept a relatively simple, uniform interface, experimenting mostly with new forms of interaction. Simple status messages and 'pokes' evolved into photos and comments. Friend requests evolved into following, and liking other content. During this time, digital platforms provided an excellent venue for social media experimentation.

User targeting helped niche social media platforms thrive. Twitter kept their original short message format as they discovered its appeal for news organizations, public relations, and celebrity followers, with short messages being supplemented with short videos and other forms of social broadcast. Pinterest attracted the interest of an older demographic by collecting images of things people wanted rather than status updates (Gilbert et al. 2013), Snapchat offered messages that disappeared after viewing, reinforcing social interaction among pre-existing small groups (Piwek and Joinson 2016), and Tumblr used a personalized blogging format to appeal to alienated teenagers wanting to express themselves, all of the above demonstrating that social media has discovered many different solutions for how to keep users engaged and interacting with each other.

Attracting investor interest was rarely a challenge for early social media sites, particularly Facebook. Rapid user growth was well-matched to the expectations of high-risk capital investors. Consistent growth rates were critical to preserving investor patience with the lack of early revenue. The prospect of rising equity values was enough to attract the technical talent and other complementary services needed to fuel rapidly growing social media sites. Advertisers in the initial stages were excited about access to desirable demographics, especially with the amount of time students were spending on social media. Given the power of freely available open software for databases and web pages, there was little need to satisfy technical partners in order to offer social media, even on a large scale.

Keeping regulators cooperating with the business model was potentially a big mobilization challenge. Social media representations build detailed portfolios of personally identifiable information about millions of people, so keeping privacy regulators on board is critical to the business model. Social media began with an ethos of voluntary sharing, which, at first, did not attract the attention of privacy regulators. Despite early discussions of social media activity possibly being used in employee hiring and firing decisions, or in school admissions decisions, regulators have largely avoided injecting themselves into the business practices of Facebook and others. In the US, the minimal privacy protections from the activity of private corporations, as opposed to government, would have to be substantially updated and upgraded in order to affect social media practices, and, so far, political mobilization in this area has not become a widespread movement. Existing regulations focus on the potential harm from selling personally identifiable information to third parties, not other concerns, and platforms like Facebook seem to prefer keeping their unique information for their own purposes.

The solution to privacy regulation offered by Facebook is largely a technical one. By providing elaborate privacy control mechanisms, social media platforms argue that users have complete control over how information is shared, and, by implication, further regulation is unnecessary. However, the default privacy settings act as a strong but hidden influence on user behavior. Most people keep the default privacy settings, which are usually set to maximize sharing. The user control argument has so far carried the day with little controversy. It is difficult to study a case of not regulating something, but there is a story remaining to be told about how social media has been able to mostly avoid privacy controversies. Even with debates over cyberbullying on social media, there have been few calls to enforce US laws which require parental consent for any online use under the age of 13. In general, despite the integration of social media into almost every aspect of modern life, maintaining the cooperation of regulators has not been a major problem.

The final important stakeholder group for social media are the advertisers. Given the growing user base, and the growing amount of time spent on social media platforms, it was not difficult to attract initial advertiser interest. In terms of ability to target specific audiences, or get messages in front of a mass audience, the social media model has been able to consistently attract advertising revenue. The process of mobilizing stakeholders for social media has been surprisingly smooth, giving technology companies the freedom to experiment with many different business models until they found the ones that work, and the freedom to adjust their technological mediations to support that business model.

7.4 THE WEALTH EFFECTS OF SOCIAL MEDIA

The social media industry is highly concentrated, with one platform dominating social media time in most countries. In the US, 79% of adults on the Internet used Facebook in 2016 (Greenwood et al. 2016). Unlike the search industry, there are viable alternative social media sites tailored to specific demographic groups, and offering new forms of technology mediation. In the US, for example, alternatives to Facebook include Twitter, Snapchat, and LinkedIn, each occupying specific niches. Each of the alternative networks attract, at most, 30% of US adult Internet users in any given month. There are powerful winner-take-all effects from having membership concentrated in a single social media site; having more of your social network on site makes it more valuable, even if a significant number of people are willing to maintain a presence on multiple social media sites.

As of 2017, the social media industry has, in a few short years, created over $400 billion US in equity wealth. The ownership of these businesses, including Facebook, is concentrated. The early investors in Facebook, who have benefitted the most from this wealth shift, were mostly already wealthy investors from previously successful technology startups. Multiple voting tiers of shares have made it possible for the primary founder of Facebook to maintain almost complete control over these resources.

The wealth generated by social media also concentrates disproportionately in the startups acquired to maintain and extend the dominance of digitally mediated business models. Facebook was able to acquire what is now the second most popular social media site in the US, Instagram, for $1 billion US in 2012. Before acquisition, Instagram lacked any meaningful business model, but was a rapidly growing social network for photo sharing on mobile devices, an area of weakness for Facebook, which depends on photo sharing for their business model to succeed. That $1 billion was shared among only 13 employees and 9 investors (Shontell 2012). Another popular social media site for job searches,

LinkedIn, was acquired by Microsoft, further demonstrating the extent to which a single digitally mediated business could dominate via acquisition.

Messaging apps provide another example of concentrated wealth. Free person-to-person messaging services, particularly WhatsApp, became popular substitutes for text messaging on mobile phones. The dominant social media platform in the US, Facebook, tried to compete at first by building their own messaging service. When their product proved less than successful, Facebook instead acquired WhatsApp for $3 billion, a seemingly huge price for an unprofitable service. When combined with Facebook's advertising business model, however, the value of those billions of user communications can be realized. Though WhatsApp had only 55 employees when it was acquired (Metz 2015), the equity and cash created by dominant social media platforms has given them the ability to acquire any challengers, and extend their dominance.

The wages paid to technology workers in social media are attractive, and presumably highly concentrated as well. The benefits and costs of social media on the rest of the economy are difficult to estimate. One study links social media use with lower economic growth, citing an increase in information search costs due to its complex mediations of human relationships (Dell'Anno et al. 2016). There is a new industry of social media marketing experts, small but rapidly growing, who benefit from the expansion of social networks. It is possible that smaller businesses might benefit from social media more than larger companies, but there is little evidence of a general renaissance of small business, leaving social media users as the last possible beneficiary of more equally distributed wealth. Consumers do acquire an entertaining and enjoyable service for free, which is beneficial. Users might improve their own social networks in real life, as early research suggested, which could ultimately bring wealth benefits. However, the psychological benefits appear to be mixed at best. In the face of clear evidence of financial wealth concentration, there is little direct evidence of any comparable countervailing force that distributes the value captured by social media more broadly.

In conclusion, social media has evolved into a business model similar to search, but with centralized ownership and control over even more detailed personal information. The advertising model has encouraged experimentation with ever more engaging technological mediations, such as profiles and news feeds, now driven by secretive behind-the-scenes algorithms. The mediation of personal relationships as profiles and feeds has become widespread and highly adopted, and the mediation of market relationships continues to expand.

As a system for value creation and capture, the current social media model has proven powerful in its ability to create wealth. It has withstood multiple challenges to its competitiveness, even as new technology-fueled opportunities have arisen. In terms of value capture, the dominant social media platforms have proven skillful at keeping all the major stakeholders on board with their business model, including users, investors, regulators, and advertisers, while maintaining healthy profit margins for themselves.

Notes

1. See Kirkpatrick (2011) for the early history of Facebook.
2. See Steers et al. (2014), also Chou and Edge (2012).

References

Acquisti, A., & Gross, R. (2006). *Imagined communities: Awareness, information sharing, and privacy on the Facebook.* Paper presented at the International Workshop on Privacy Enhancing Technologies, Cambridge, UK.

Agarwal, D., Chen, B.-C., Gupta, R., Hartman, J., He, Q., Iyer, A., … Singh, A. (2014). *Activity ranking in LinkedIn feed.* Paper presented at the 20th ACM SIGKDD International Conference on Knowledge Discovery and Data Mining, New York.

Back, M. D., Stopfer, J. M., Vazire, S., Gaddis, S., Schmukle, S. C., Egloff, B., et al. (2010). Facebook profiles reflect actual personality, not self-idealization. *Psychological Science, 21*(3), 372–374.

Bakshy, E., Messing, S., & Adamic, L. A. (2015). Exposure to ideologically diverse news and opinion on Facebook. *Science, 348*(6239), 1130–1132.

Bucher, T. (2012). Want to be on the top? Algorithmic power and the threat of invisibility on Facebook. *New Media & Society, 14*(7), 1164–1180.

Chou, H.-T. G., & Edge, N. (2012). "They are happier and having better lives than I am": The impact of using Facebook on perceptions of others' lives. *Cyberpsychology, Behavior, and Social Networking, 15*(2), 117–121.

Dell'Anno, R., Rayna, T., & Solomon, O. H. (2016). Impact of social media on economic growth—evidence from social media. *Applied Economics Letters, 23*(9), 633–636.

Dwyer, C., Hiltz, S., & Passerini, K. (2007). *Trust and privacy concern within social networking sites: A comparison of Facebook and MySpace.* Paper presented at the 2007 Americas Conference on Information Systems, Keystone, CO.

Ellison, N. B., Steinfield, C., & Lampe, C. (2007). The benefits of Facebook "friends": Social capital and college students' use of online social network sites. *Journal of Computer-Mediated Communication, 12*(4), 1143–1168.

Facebook. (2017). Facebook—Financials. Retrieved February 6, 2017, from https://investor.fb.com/financials/?section=secfilings.

Gilbert, E., Bakhshi, S., Chang, S., & Terveen, L. (2013). *I need to try this? A statistical overview of pinterest.* Paper presented at the SIGCHI Conference on Human Factors In Computing Systems, Paris.

Greenwood, S., Perrin, A., & Duggan, M. (2016). Social media update 2016. Retrieved February 16, 2017, from http://www.pewinternet.org/2016/11/11/social-media-update-2016/.

Kirkpatrick, D. (2011). *The Facebook effect: The inside story of the company that is connecting the world.* New York: Simon and Schuster.

Marichal, J. (2016). *Facebook democracy: The architecture of disclosure and the threat to public life.* London: Routledge.

Marshall, T. C., Lefringhausen, K., & Ferenczi, N. (2015). The Big Five, self-esteem, and narcissism as predictors of the topics people write about in Facebook status updates. *Personality and Individual Differences, 85,* 35–40.

Mehdizadeh, S. (2010). Self-presentation 2.0: Narcissism and self-esteem on Facebook. *Cyberpsychology, Behavior, and Social Networking, 13*(4), 357–364.

Metz, C. (2015). Why WhatsApp only needs 50 engineers for its 900 million users. Retrieved February 16, 2017, from https://www.wired.com/2015/09/whatsapp-serves-900-million-users-50-engineers/.

Pempek, T. A., Yermolayeva, Y. A., & Calvert, S. L. (2009). College students' social networking experiences on Facebook. *Journal of Applied Developmental Psychology, 30*(3), 227–238.

Piwek, L., & Joinson, A. (2016). "What do they snapchat about?" Patterns of use in time-limited instant messaging service. *Computers in Human Behavior, 54,* 358–367.

Sagioglou, C., & Greitemeyer, T. (2014). Facebook's emotional consequences: Why Facebook causes a decrease in mood and why people still use it. *Computers in Human Behavior, 35,* 359–363.

Sheldon, P., & Bryant, K. (2016). Instagram: Motives for its use and relationship to narcissism and contextual age. *Computers in Human Behavior, 58,* 89–97.

Shontell, A. (2012). Meet the 13 lucky employees and 9 investors behind $1 billion Instagram. Retrieved February 16, 2017, from http://www.businessinsider.com/instagram-employees-and-investors-2012-4.

Steers, M.-L. N., Wickham, R. E., & Acitelli, L. K. (2014). Seeing everyone else's highlight reels: How Facebook usage is linked to depressive symptoms. *Journal of Social and Clinical Psychology, 33*(8), 701–731.

Zhao, S., Grasmuck, S., & Martin, J. (2008). Identity construction on Facebook: Digital empowerment in anchored relationships. *Computers in Human Behavior, 24*(5), 1816–1836.

CHAPTER 8

Technology and Inequality Case Study: The Sharing Economy

Abstract Using the four-part framework of mediation, model, mobilization, and wealth effects, we analyze the case of the sharing economy. The digital technology used to mediate the sharing economy platforms has evolved to attract and maintain the trust of a diversity of buyers and sellers, while meeting the expectations of multi-billion dollar investors. The sharing economy model was often in conflict with local regulations when it began, so developing a capacity for regulatory change has been a key mobilization challenge. In contrast to its communitarian roots, the business model of the sharing economy has raised massive amounts of capital from wealthy investors, but has yet to create substantial operating profits. The ultimate effects on wealth inequality remain to be seen, but evidence of significant wealth decentralization is difficult to find.

Keywords Sharing economy · Uber · Airbnb · Venture capital · Business models

8.1 Digital Mediation of the Sharing Economy

The sharing economy is still a bit too young to define precisely, but generally incorporates a variety of sites that connect non-traditional providers of goods and services with buyers or recipients. The services offered could be a shared room in a home (instead of a hotel), a car ride (instead of a taxi or public transit), or simply the giving away of an unneeded item for free. Any concept that incorporates both multi-billion dollar venture-backed firms like Uber and the local neighborhood seed bank is in danger of stretching beyond the breaking point, but the vision is coherent enough to have attracted incredible consumer, media, and investor interest (Schor 2016).

The sharing economy has been described as an extension of the peer-to-peer sharing ethos of the digital world to goods and services in the physical world (Hamari et al. 2015). An earlier term for this idea, 'collaborative consumption,' emphasized the community roots in this vision of people sharing their own things, and themselves, rather than turning to commercial businesses. Botsman famously tied this communitarian (and somewhat anti-consumerist) notion to the idea that many privately owned assets, such as cars and houses, have low utilization. Her examples of power drills only used for 10 min or so in their lifetimes, or of automobiles laying idle over 90% of the time (Botsman and Rogers 2010), brought together three powerful images: community sharing, reduced environmental impact, and lower cost services when those unused assets were shared. Creating a business model around power drill sharing proved to be too difficult (Kessler 2015), but the phenomenal rise of companies such as Airbnb and Uber speaks to the power of extending markets to non-traditional sellers.

The key digital mediation choices for sharing economy sites revolve around two closely related challenges. As a two-sided market, the technology has to attract, and match, both providers and consumers, and the technology needs to facilitate this match in a way enticing to both sides. The second challenge is to maintain trust. Goods and services provided by community members, rather than businesses, require entering into a different kind of relationship. Staying in someone's bedroom requires a different type of trust than checking into a hotel. Sharing economy sites provide representations of providers and consumers, often in the form of online reviews.

The matching function of sharing economy sites faces a tension between consumer convenience and community control. With mobile devices, digital technology offers the possibility of always available services at the push of a button, and a seamless payment experience completely handled online. This was the original vision of Uber's founders, as they waited for a taxi on a rainy night in Paris (Wirtz and Tang 2016). To maximize consumer convenience in sharing economy services such as a car rides, many drivers need to be on the road, and those drivers need to accept requests for service. Car ride services such as Uber and Lyft allow drivers to accept or reject rides, but incentivize drivers to accept more requests through bonuses for high-acceptance rates, and sanctions for lower acceptance rates. Uber and Lyft differ in their mediations of tips, with Uber preferring the more seamless interaction of no tipping through the system, while Lyft explicitly asks passengers if they would like to include a tip.

The home-sharing site Airbnb offers two different mediations of match acceptance. The most common interaction is to request a booking, which the provider reviews and accepts about half of the time. The other representation is an instant booking function, which decreases the control providers have, but makes the process more like a seamless consumer purchase. Not much is known about the algorithm through which search rankings are created on Airbnb.

The mediation of human-to-human relationships for building trust consists of personal profiles, and online reviews. One of the claimed benefits of sharing economy marketplaces is the removal of information asymmetries. Through elaborate ratings and profile information, consumers and providers should know much more about each other, making markets more effective (Koopman et al. 2014). Most sharing economy sites use bi-directional reviews, with consumers and providers both rating each other. Service providers who fall below a certain average rating on Uber or Lyft will either be suspended or dismissed by the system, while Airbnb relies on consumers to make their own judgments. The challenge with bi-directional reviewing, however, is that average rankings tend to be very high, with little variance. 95% of Airbnb ratings are either 4.5 out of 5 stars or above, with an average score of 4.7 (Zervas et al. Forthcoming). The same properties reviewed on another site with reviews only by customers, TripAdvisor, had lower scores and higher variance, making the information more useful. There appears to be some fear of retaliation and underreporting of negative experiences, which can erode trust on sharing economy platforms.

The other key mediation challenge is the use of real names, particularly in bi-directional reviews. If the non-traditional service providers are given the choice of accepting offers or not, consumers can be subject to ethnic and gender discrimination. One study of Airbnb found people with African American sounding names saw their identical booking requests rejected 16% more often.[1] Another study found that African American sounding names were more likely to see their ride requests rejected by Uber and Lyft drivers,[2] and when photos are included in profiles 75% of customers prefer a female host (Ge et al. 2016). The discrimination issue became serious enough to inspire Airbnb to send a message to all users in 2016 reaffirming their anti-discrimination policies. Interestingly, one proposed representation change to reduce discrimination is to share less information, by using account names rather than real names, and to give providers less control over which requests they accept, by increasing the use of instant booking technologies (Ert et al. 2016).

Most of the representations in sharing economy sites mediate person-to-person relationships, but there are also interesting mediations of the person-to-world relationship. For early customers of ride-sharing companies, graphical representations of cars on maps gave users the impression many drivers were available to give them a ride. In the earliest stages of ride sharing, however, cars on the screen were not always physically there, but were only a representation to give users a general idea that many drivers were nearby (Allen 2016). To entice drivers, the sharing economy platforms provided heat maps showing areas of high demand, and sent automated messages during busy times. When simple tools were created to show drivers their earnings, costs such as insurance, gasoline, and taxes were omitted from the calculation. The technology mediations are constantly evolving to persuade both sides of the market through strong messages and more hidden influence.

For the representations that match consumers and providers, and the rating mechanisms that create trust in non-traditional markets, we see a range of fundamental mediation choices. As sharing economy platforms balance the needs of their business model, with its many stakeholders, there are choices to be made that reflect different possibilities. What appeared to be a simple case of letting community members find each other has become entwined with perhaps one of the most complicated business models ever seen.

8.2 The Sharing Economy Business Model

The business model of the largest sharing economy sites has converged on three basic elements. First, the sharing economy business takes a transaction fee, typically ranging from 15 to 30%. Second, the business tries to avoid liability for transactions by claiming that they merely connect buyers and sellers, and do not provide services themselves. Third, the revenue shares for providers and the mediating company can vary in real time, both in terms of variable pricing service, and the percentage of fees or bonuses service providers receive.

In contrast with search and social media, the sharing economy has converged on a transaction-based business model. Compared to other classic intermediaries in the past, such as real estate brokers and travel agents, the transaction fees commanded by sharing economy business are quite substantial. In terms of value capture, transactions are relatively easy to implement when matching buyers and sellers, as long as there are no convenient ways for the two sides to complete a transaction after finding each other on a platform. Sharing economy platforms only reveal the match after the transaction is agreed to, making it difficult to back out and complete their transaction outside the system.

Just as important to the sharing economy business model is the limitation of risk, or liability. For the major ride-sharing and room-sharing companies, their business models could not function if they complied with the same liability regulations as competitors such as taxis and hotels. Ride-sharing companies like Uber and Lyft have fought hard to maintain the legal classification of drivers as independent contractors rather than employees (Cunningham-Parmeter 2016), with more success in the US than in other countries. In traditional customer-business relationships, US law recognizes that commercial entities often have increased liability because of their superior knowledge of safety issues, or uneven bargaining power (Katz 2015). Tenants, for example, have rights to a habitable building, evictions only through due process, and non-discrimination. With the new relationship created by sharing economy platforms, the duties of the commercial party are now in many ways shared between the platform and the service provider. Until the law is clarified, sharing economy businesses will seek to impose this liability on their service providers to the full extent public relations will allow. These companies do claim to provide a level of safety and security, but this is in tension with their need to avoid liability.

A third area of business model innovation, pioneered by the ride-sharing platforms, has been variable pricing. With real-time information about both service provider availability and customer requests, sharing economy platforms are in the uniquely powerful position of being able to vary prices due to shifts in supply and demand on a real-time basis. How much do prices need to increase before drivers will get in their cars to meet surging demand? How many special discounts have to be offered to keep customers using the platform? In terms of acquisition costs, how much of an inducement is required to sign up a sufficient number of new drivers and new customers?

In these two-sided markets, the customer value proposition has to apply to both the consumers and the service providers. For consumers, the value proposition has fluctuated between the benefits of community interaction, and more commercial considerations of price and convenience. For car rides, Lyft in the US began as a true ride-sharing company with neighbors, while Uber began as a pure on-demand limousine service. Over time, the two companies have converged to a very similar business model, one more oriented toward customer values of low price and convenience. Even sharing economy sites that begin as completely free and community-driven have a tendency to become more commercially oriented over time (Martin et al. 2015). The prospect of cheaper, more convenient car trips and room booking has kept increasing numbers of customers buying into the value proposition.

For service providers, the value proposition of additional income through sharing their assets and expertize has had more mixed success. Airbnb has had little difficulty attracting more rooms to their platform than even the largest traditional hotel chain, and the number of hosts keeps growing (Cusumano 2015). For car ride services, driver turnover has been much higher, forcing companies to spend much more in driver bonuses in order to retain service providers.

For sharing economy companies, their position as a digitally mediated market has allowed them to experiment with their business models in real time, and build a stockpile of personally identifiable information that is kept to themselves. The car ride companies can change their variable prices and bonus incentives to see how much inducement is required to attract both sides of the market, but exactly how much money is required to get a sufficient number of drivers out on the streets? How much of a price increase will consumers accept before requests disappear? The business model experiments, for the most part, have been trying to find the right formula for sharing revenue among consumers, service providers, and the company themselves, but there are now experiments with extensions to the model, such as deliveries, events, and additional services. Constant experimentation has been necessary in order to find the exact business model that will meet the revenue expectations of all their stakeholders, in particular the investors who have bet billions of dollars on these startups. Unlike the early days of search engines and social media, building large sharing economy platforms has been an expensive business, requiring serious financial resources.

8.3 Mobilizing for the Sharing Economy

Even more than search or social media, sharing economy sites have had to master the art of keeping multiple parties with different interests on board while at the same time fending off powerful competition. At their most basic, sharing economy businesses are two-sided markets, needing to attract both the consumers or buyers of services, and the sellers or service providers. In two-sided markets, the classic dilemma is to what extent one side or the other needs to cross-subsidize in order to attract both (Rochet and Tirole 2003). A sharing platform could be subsidized or free for service providers at the expense of the end customers, or vice versa—yet finding the right mix of cross-subsidy can be tricky, and, in some cases, not even possible if both sides of the market coordinate their actions. As relatively new business models, sharing economy businesses need to experiment and search for the right mix of inducements.

For any new digital business that depends on a critical mass of users, building that critical mass from zero is challenging. For two-sided markets, two different communities with different interests have to be simultaneously brought to critical mass, an even greater challenge. Search business models did not face this extreme critical mass challenge because they could leverage an already existing critical mass of web content at first. Social media, like most community-driven technologies, did face an initial critical mass problem, and found success at first with a phased rollout strategy, building a critical mass in limited geographic areas first and then expanding. Sharing economy businesses have used a similar strategy.

Because the vision of the sharing economy includes environmental and community benefits as well as economic ones, researchers have examined whether consumers and service providers are attracted to sharing economy sites for primarily economic gain, or other reasons. Customers tend to treat the sharing economy sites instrumentally, with utility, cost effectiveness, and familiarity being the main issues that make them more likely to use these services (Möhlmann 2015). For the service providers, though, the main attraction seems to be for 'microbusiness' entrepreneurs trying to take advantage of a new economic opportunity (Sundararajan 2016). The service providers themselves spend much time and effort discussing whether part-time 'gigs' and 'side hustles' actually pay off economically, with some consensus that sharing economy jobs are better for part-time work under special circumstances rather than being an effective full-time job (Oei and Ring 2016). Over time, the major ride-sharing companies have increased their fees and reduced the overall wage rate paid to drivers. So far, preserving the original sharing economy vision of community relationships has not been necessary to keep the growing numbers of consumers and service providers on board.

In terms of purely economic cross-subsidy, however, the large sharing economy sites have brought a third party to the table: high-risk capital investors. Uber in particular has raised over $9 billion US from early stage and venture capital investors, probably more than any other startup in history. Thanks to this huge investment, Uber has been able to withstand estimated losses of over $3 billion US in 2016 alone, with much of that money being used to subsidize driver payments and customer discounts. Their main competitor, Lyft, limited their losses in 2016 to a relatively healthy $50 million US per month. These resources to subsidize both sides of the sharing economy markets have been used to accelerate user growth, fueling a global rollout in just a few short years. Unless potential competitors can also subsidize their two-sided markets at a rate of hundreds of millions of dollars per year, they are unlikely to be able to compete.

In exchange for providing these massive capital inflows, the high risk investors bring with them expectations that must be met to keep them on board. The user growth rates and market size has to be maintained at a magnitude that can justify billion dollar levels of investment. This demands a constant search for new markets, with rapid expansion either geographically or into related services such as deliveries, putting constant pressure on the sharing economy platforms to grow.

On top of all this mobilization complexity comes the most significant challenge of all, satisfying the regulators. Markets such as room rentals and car transportation have long-established and heavily regulated competition. To what extent the sharing economy platforms are direct substitutes for traditional taxi and hotel industries is still a matter of debate. One study of Austin, Texas found a hotel revenue decrease of only 0.05% for every 1% increase in Airbnb revenue (Zervas et al. Forthcoming). Another study in Idaho found a marginal decrease in low-end hotel employment once Airbnb penetration reached a certain size (Fang et al. 2016). In San Francisco, the arrival of the ride-sharing industry reduced taxi trips by 65% in 18 months (Bond 2014).

Compared to hotels and taxis, the sharing economy platforms had the initial advantage of not complying with existing regulations. Sharing economy drivers were not employees but independent contractors, and did not obey taxi regulations such as driver background checks, safety inspections, and mandatory service for people with disabilities. Room-sharing sites did not obey hotel regulations, bypassing local taxes and safety regulations. Airbnb rentals were often illegal in cities with restrictions on short-term rentals.[3] Existing companies insisted that they needed to compete on a 'level playing field,' with sharing economy platforms conforming to the same regulations they were subject to, while the sharing platform companies argued that they were fundamentally new and different, and simply connected people to each other rather than provided services themselves.

The new sharing platforms have been relatively successful so far at getting regulators to agree that they should be defined as something new and different. In California, Uber and Lyft were able to convince local regulators to create a new category of company: a transportation network, or TNC, which is subject to different regulations than taxi companies. Local government lobbying has become a key strategic capability to enable their expansion plans, with companies such as Uber hiring the most expensive lobbyists, and creating a rollout strategy for removing local opposition. Part of the strategy involves local consumers and service providers testifying to the superior service and lower cost of sharing economy platforms. The sharing economy companies emphasize how additional income helps contribute to middle-class wages, or allows struggling middle-class homeowners to stay in their homes, but these strategies have become less effective as the number of full-time commercial operators increase on sharing platforms, such as the Airbnb hosts who manage multiple properties and buy new ones to use as short-term rentals. In contrast, countries outside the US have been more eager to enforce existing regulations for car rides and room rentals.

Sharing economy companies have been surprisingly successful at mobilizing a complex set of actors in two key markets: car rides and room rentals. But the complexity of this juggling act can be measured by the lack of sharing economy alternatives in other areas. The complex mobilization is difficult to pull off, and apparently requires a level of investment beyond the reach of most entrepreneurs. Despite initial associations with frugality and more efficient resource use, the sharing economy is turning out to be a very expensive business model.

8.4 The Wealth Effects of the Sharing Economy

The wealth effects of the sharing economy are difficult to calculate. Many of the costs and benefits of these activities are broad estimates, and the privately held companies at its center are not required to share their financial information. For its highly concentrated and wealthy initial investors, the largest sharing economy companies have created a lot of wealth on paper. As of the end of 2016, Uber raised about $9 billion US of venture capital in 14 funding rounds, with 53 major investors (Crunchbase 2017), which has so far produced a valuation of over $60 billion US, but to what extent this will be realized as actual equity wealth remains to be seen. Their main competitor, Lyft, raised $2 billion US in nine funding rounds from 30 major investors, producing a valuation of about $5 billion US, and Airbnb raised $3 billion US, producing a $30 billion US valuation. For a movement that began with a hippie ethos, the sharing economy has become a hotbed of the most hardcore capitalists around.

What is less clear is how the service providers have benefitted. Is the sharing economy providing a much needed lifeline at a time of middle-class wage stagnation? Or is it more a case of desperation asset stripping, working for less than minimum wage and wearing down their own assets? For Sundararajan and others, the main benefit of the sharing economy is its democratization of economic opportunity, providing a potentially new way for the digital world to reduce inequality. He points to millions of part-time sellers on the craft site Etsy as evidence of the power of microbusiness entrepreneurs. According to his research, room-sharing hosts are disproportionately from lower income households (Sundararajan 2016). A single platform, Uber, pays around $2.5 billion US in fees per year to drivers while losing billions themselves. The effective pay rate for ride-sharing drivers on Lyft has been estimated at $11–14 US per hour in most of the country, but around $29 US per hour in New York (Wirtz and Tang 2016). A study of the spread of Airbnb in London argues that hosts are about evenly split between room rentals from younger, less wealthy workers in tourist-friendly locations, and more financially secure homeowners who rent out their entire properties (Quattrone et al. 2016). Future studies will need to look more closely at the different effects sharing platforms have on different categories of service providers.

In online discussions, drivers on sharing economy platforms have difficulty justifying the purchase of an automobile specifically for giving rides, but can see situations where using older cars and driving part-time could pay off economically (Allen 2016). If driving doesn't pay for a fully costed car with insurance and depreciation, then service providers are likely using up their own assets for the benefit of sharing economy companies. On Airbnb, in contrast, the number of listings by investors who specifically purchase and manage properties for short-term rentals seems to be growing.

For consumers, the benefits of additional convenience and lower cost are substantial, assuming that they are not discriminated against due to ethnicity or physical disability. Cohen and colleagues use data on accepted and rejected ride offers using variable pricing to estimate that $7 billion US of consumer surplus value was generated in 2015 alone (Cohen et al. 2016). The ride-sharing platforms are burning through investor cash at an unprecedented rate, and much of this is winding up in the pockets of the consumer. Whether this is sustainable over time remains to be seen. Airbnb, in contrast, has now reached the point of not having to subsidize consumers with discounts.

There is still much debate over the costs and benefits for sharing economy companies on communities as a whole. What are the negative, and positive, externalities of sharing platforms? Are ride-sharing platforms more dangerous because of fewer safety regulations, background checks, and less insurance? One recent study in the US found no significant changes with the rollout of Uber across the country either positively, in terms of reduced drunk driving, or negatively, in terms of increased accidents or fatalities (Brazil and Kirk 2016). Despite the theoretical advantages of driving underutilized cars as a way of improving resource use, a recent regulatory filing argues that traffic congestion has increased in San Francisco's downtown core by 30–40% due to ride-sharing drivers (Reiskin 2016).

It is thought that room-sharing platforms might be taking rental housing away from local residents so would-be landlords can make more money using them as hotels. Is this, in fact, occurring? If so, would operating a housing business in residential neighborhoods have negative consequences for local residents, such as increased noise, or a smaller base of permanent residents to attract the services they need? Airbnb's own studies argue that room-sharing visitors stay two days longer on average than regular hotel visitors, and spend more money outside the usual tourist core (Guttentag 2015) whereas Quattrone and colleagues (2016) found Airbnb rentals did spread somewhat from London's tourist core over time, but still remained highly concentrated.

In terms of contributing back to the economy through taxation, sharing economy platforms have likely reduced overall tax collection. In their early stages, the platforms contrasted with older industries that paid more taxes, such as mandatory hotel taxes levied on visitors. As the sharing companies have grown so have political demands to tax them. Ride-sharing companies are now usually required to pay local taxes such as airport fees, but, in the US, have not been required to pay employee payroll taxes because of their special regulatory status. Room-sharing platforms like Airbnb are increasingly required by local governments to collect local hotel or short-stay rental taxes, but this is only in few cities where they have faced political pressure, and most estimates assume that sharing economy platforms have paid fewer taxes than the industries that came before them.

Looking at the sharing economy as a whole, we see one of the most complex digitally mediated business models ever attempted. The technology standing between buyers and sellers provides ample opportunities for experimentation based on unique data and scaling to large populations. Much of this experimentation is driven by the need to mobilize powerful outside constituents, particularly early investors and regulators. Somewhat surprisingly, the communitarian and environmental vision of asset and service sharing has now become an industry concentrated on only a very few areas (car rides and room rentals) based on a business model that requires massive capital investment and correspondingly high financial returns. The model has had difficulty spreading to the sharing of expertise, or power drills.

Most of the wealth created by the sharing economy has yet to be realized, but, if it is successful, the wealth created will be highly concentrated in the hands of technology founders and early investors, and public infrastructure will likely receive slightly less funding. The benefits for consumers have been substantial, but for communities as a whole is more mixed and deserves further investigation. The most controversial part of the equation is the wealth effect on service providers. The platforms create a gray area of service provision, somewhere between helpful neighbors and commercial businesses, and it is not yet clear who will benefit the most from the new arrangements. Amidst the uncertainty, we see some evidence of the increase in economic opportunity implied by the early vision of the sharing economy, but perhaps not enough to offset the concentration in business wealth from these large startups.

NOTES

1. See Edelman et al. (Forthcoming). The ethnic disparity for accepting booking requests disappears when the Airbnb host has at least one review from an African American guest on their profile.
2. See Ge et al. (2016). Female riders in Boston were also taken for longer rides.
3. The 'success' of startups like Airbnb that relied on illegal behavior at the beginning has been annoying for teachers of entrepreneurship. Now students are asking us, why do our new business ideas have to be legal?

REFERENCES

Allen, J. P. (2016). *The sharing economy: Studying technology-mediated social movements.* Paper presented at the 2016 ACM SIGMIS Conference on Computers and People Research, Alexandria, VA.

Bond, A. T. (2014). An app for that: Local governments and the rise of the sharing economy. *Notre Dame Law Review Online, 90,* 77.

Botsman, R., & Rogers, R. (2010). *What's mine is yours: How collaborative consumption is changing the way we live.* New York: HarperCollins.

Brazil, N., & Kirk, D. S. (2016). Uber and metropolitan traffic fatalities in the United States. *American Journal of Epidemiology, 184*(3), 192–198.

Cohen, P., Hahn, R., Hall, J., Levitt, S., & Metcalfe, R. (2016). Using big data to estimate consumer surplus: The case of Uber. Retrieved February 17, 2017, from http://www.nber.org/papers/w22627.

Crunchbase. (2017). Uber. Retrieved February 17, 2017, from https://www.crunchbase.com/organization/uber-/entity.

Cunningham-Parmeter, K. (2016). From Amazon to Uber: Defining employment in the modern economy. *Boston University Law Review, 96,* 1673.

Cusumano, M. A. (2015). How traditional firms must compete in the sharing economy. *Communications of the ACM, 58*(1), 32–34.

Edelman, B., Luca, M., & Svirsky, D. (Forthcoming). Racial discrimination in the sharing economy: Evidence from a field experiment. *American Economic Journal: Applied Economics.*

Ert, E., Fleischer, A., & Magen, N. (2016). Trust and reputation in the sharing economy: The role of personal photos in Airbnb. *Tourism Management, 55,* 62–73.

Fang, B., Ye, Q., & Law, R. (2016). Effect of sharing economy on tourism industry employment. *Annals of Tourism Research, 57,* 264–267.

Ge, Y., Knittel, C. R., MacKenzie, D., & Zoepf, S. (2016). Racial and gender discrimination in transportation network companies. Retrieved February 17, 2017, from http://www.nber.org/papers/w22776.

Guttentag, D. (2015). Airbnb: Disruptive innovation and the rise of an informal tourism accommodation sector. *Current Issues in Tourism, 18*(12), 1192–1217.

Hamari, J., Sjöklint, M., & Ukkonen, A. (2015). The sharing economy: Why people participate in collaborative consumption. *Journal of the Association for Information Science and Technology, 67*(9), 2047–2059.

Katz, V. (2015). Regulating the sharing economy. *Berkeley Technology Law Journal, 30,* 1067.

Kessler, S. (2015). The 'sharing economy' is dead, and we killed it. *Fast Company.* Retrieved February 17, 2017, from https://www.fastcompany.com/3050775/the-sharing-economy-is-dead-and-we-killed-it.

Koopman, C., Mitchell, M., & Thierer, A. (2014). The sharing economy and consumer protection regulation: The case for policy change. *Journal of Business Entrepreneurship and Law, 8,* 529.

Martin, C. J., Upham, P., & Budd, L. (2015). Commercial orientation in grassroots social innovation: Insights from the sharing economy. *Ecological Economics, 118,* 240–251.

Möhlmann, M. (2015). Collaborative consumption: Determinants of satisfaction and the likelihood of using a sharing economy option again. *Journal of Consumer Behaviour, 14*(3), 193–207.

Oei, S.-Y., & Ring, D. M. (2016). The tax lives of Uber drivers: Evidence from internet discussion forums. Retrieved February 17, 2017, from https://papers.ssrn.com/sol3/papers2.cfm?abstract_id=2730893.

Quattrone, G., Proserpio, D., Quercia, D., Capra, L., & Musolesi, M. (2016). *Who Benefits from the Sharing Economy of Airbnb?* Paper presented at the 25th International World Wide Web Conference, Montréal, Canada.

Reiskin, E. D. (2016). Comments of San Francisco municipal transportation agency on proposed decision for phase iii.a: Definition of personal vehicle. Retrieved February 17, 2017, from http://docs.cpuc.ca.gov/PublishedDocs/Efile/G000/M170/K774/170774103.PDF.

Rochet, J. C., & Tirole, J. (2003). Platform competition in two-sided markets. *Journal of the European Economic Association, 1*(4), 990–1029.

Schor, J. (2016). Debating the sharing economy. *Journal of Self-Governance and Management Economics, 4*(3), 7–22.

Sundararajan, A. (2016). *The sharing economy: The end of employment and the rise of crowd-based capitalism.* Cambridge, MA: MIT Press.

Wirtz, J., & Tang, C. (2016). Uber: Competing as market leader in the US versus being a distant second in China. In J. Wirtz & C. H. Lovelock (Eds.), *Services marketing: People, technology, strategy* (pp. 626–632). Singapore: World Scientific Publishing..

Zervas, G., Proserpio, D., & Byers, J. W. (Forthcoming). The rise of the sharing economy: Estimating the impact of Airbnb on the hotel industry. *Journal of Marketing Research.* http://journals.ama.org/doi/abs/10.1509/jmr.15.0204?code=amma-site

CHAPTER 9

Restoring Technology as an Engine of Opportunity

Abstract This chapter uses what we have learned about technology and inequality to find new opportunities for reducing inequality in a more digital world. Our key strategy is to focus on the ways financial value is created by the digital technology sector, and the specific ways that value is captured. Digitally mediated markets are a new and growing phenomenon, and new digital business models have created valuable products and services through their unprecedented abilities to experiment, amass unique data, and deploy to huge populations, offering new ways to capture and concentrate that value on a seemingly unprecedented scale. Inequality can be addressed through the remedies proposed by the technological and institutional context schools, but we think these will be incomplete without paying attention to the business models being used to deploy these technologies. Specific technological mediation choices, or the mobilization of stakeholders that technologies depend on, may be part of the strategy, but these issues in the end always return to the question of how to invent alternative business models that will share the value captured more evenly. Whatever path we choose, the wealth shifts associated with digital technology are too large to ignore if we want to seriously reverse increasing inequality and create more widespread opportunity.

Keywords Digital technology · Technology and inequality · Technology and opportunity · Wealth concentration · Digital mediation

9.1 Digital Technology as an 'Engine of Opportunity'

In this book, we have focused on the role of digital technology in creating a world of severe economic inequality. Severe economic inequality has been associated with many negative social outcomes, including economic stagnation, lower social mobility, greater division and polarization in society, and even negative health effects. Thanks to the work of Piketty, Stiglitz, and others, rising inequality has become a wider academic and political issue. But an even more important reason for studying economic inequality is that it provides a practical way to examine some of the biggest anxieties in modern developed societies. Is there still economic opportunity for the middle class? Or was the middle class an aberration in human history, a temporary product of a 'golden age' never to be repeated? Will future generations be better off? Is modern society truly fair and just? Where will the political desire, and financial resources, come from to save our planet from environmental collapse?

At the start of the book, our goal was to restore technology to an 'engine of opportunity,' but what does this really mean? Opportunity is about possibilities, which are difficult, if not impossible, to study directly. Finding opportunities that can be exploited commercially is at the heart of definitions of entrepreneurship (Shane 2003), and perhaps business more generally, but opportunity, in this sense, can only be measured indirectly through data such as new business formation or self-employment, whereas intergenerational social mobility studies define opportunity as the likelihood of moving into a higher socioeconomic level than one's parents (Breen 2004).

We focus on Sen's definition of opportunity as practical freedom (Sen 1999). Practical freedom means living above the poverty level, with access to health care and educational opportunities. It means having the resources and capabilities needed for people to live their lives in the way they choose. The resources are often economic, but can also be based on social relationships: one can pay someone to paint their house, or get family and friends to help them. Practical freedom is, in essence, the definition of middle-class life.

Sen deliberately refused to create a universal definition of practical freedom, claiming that freedom reflects human values, and that each community should define their own values through local political processes. Nevertheless, Sen's definition has been used to create the United Nations Human Development Index (HDI), which defines life opportunities at the national level by combining measures of per capita Gross Domestic Product (for wealth), longevity (for health), and literacy rate (for education) (Anand and Sen 1994). Even though wealth is only one component of opportunity, we focus on it because of the high correlations between wealth, education, and health in the developed world. These correlations, however, are not perfect—a poor, but educated person might spot a new opportunity that would otherwise be missed, or an unhealthy person might have drastically reduced life possibilities, even if they are wealthy. With the increasing financialization of economies, however, access to financial wealth is now more than ever a resource for opportunity. The wealthy tend to have better developed social networks, and even tend to match with similarly connected marriage partners. The correlations between wealth and life opportunity are dependent on changes in society at large. As health care and education become more a function of ability to pay rather than universal access wealth becomes a stronger indicator of life possibilities. The great wealth shift to financial assets in the information technology and finance sectors is the key pathway for examining the connection between digital technology and growing wealth inequality.

The development of digital technology has come in historical phases, starting with large mainframe computers and extending to personal computers, the Internet, mobile devices and networks all the way to today's artificial intelligence and big data. For those, like me, who were brought up in the era of the personal computer and the Internet, we expect technology to be an instrument of liberation, that digital technology should distribute life opportunities, and ultimately, wealth, more evenly. For those of us brought up in the eras of mobile technology, AI and big data, expectations for technology-driven opportunity might not be as strong. Today's debate about robots and job loss is more a return to a discussion about the threats of automation as a direct substitute for human labor, rather than a debate about how to maximize opportunity.

Whatever the specific expectations about digital technology and human opportunity, in general technology is supposed to be an instrument that furthers human capabilities. This is true of each of the two main models of technology's effect on the world: technology as an outside force that brings progress and change, improving human life; and technology as a tool that forwards our designs and desires. There is a deep, unforgivable irony to the notion of technology hindering human progress and development. If technology is playing a role in growing inequality, it is important to understand it, and reverse it. Information technology gives humanity unprecedented capabilities to create, to remember, and to share with each other, to be more knowledgeable and less dependent on limited physical resources. These are capabilities that every human being can benefit from. These sources of value should absolutely be an engine of opportunity that is widely shared throughout society.

9.2 The Information Technology Sector: Key Questions of Value Creation and Value Capture

The key empirical phenomena with which we begin our investigation is what we call 'The Great Wealth Shift'. Since 1980, in the developed economies and particularly in the United States, wealth has shifted to the virtual economy of financial assets, especially in the information technology and finance sectors. This can be seen as a kind of virtualized economy, where the economic sectors that traditionally have assisted the 'real' economy have increasingly become the actual economy themselves. Finance, which is supposed to help the real economy make good resource allocation decisions, has become a major economic sector in its own right. And information technology, whose traditional economic role has been to provide better information or insight about real economic activity in order to make better decisions, has become a major economic sector itself.

In terms of the wealth generated by different economic sectors, the market value of finance and IT has increased dramatically since 1980, from about 10% to 40% of the stock market capitalization of large companies in the US, while energy and materials have declined from about 40% to 10%, with the rest of the real economy staying at roughly half the amount of market capitalization. A 30% shift in large company market capitalization represents a $6–9 trillion US dollar wealth shift, an amount large enough to account for substantial changes in wealth inequality.

As part of this virtualized economy, more buyers and sellers are connected through markets that are digitally mediated Unlike the classic theory of perfect markets, mediated markets are run by technology companies that have their own business models. These large technology companies operate through unique data sets and secretive algorithms rather than through the information sharing and full transparency of traditional free markets. Their digital business models can be understood by separating two important concepts: value creation and value capture. Digital companies in particular have become very creative in their discovery and optimization of new business models, even in non-technological industries.

After investigating digital technology and wealth shifts in search, social media, and the sharing economy, even with the limited knowledge we have, our hypothesis is that the largest technology companies have become extremely skilled in optimizing their business models to increase the value created, and, just as importantly, the value captured. Anywhere that new technology comes into contact with buyers or sellers digital business models have three fundamental advantages for value capture: experimentation, exclusive data, and scalability. Technology companies have unprecedented ability to experiment with the business models that will keep diverse sets of buyers, sellers, investors, regulators, and employees on board while maximizing the value being captured.

The same experimental skills used throughout industry, such as A/B testing, are amplified by the major technology platforms. A major platform such as Google or Netflix might run thousands of experiments a day. With their ability to fine-tune their performance, they can adjust their entire business model, not just a specific product. And with the scalability of digital technology, combined with their already massive customer reach, the big technology platforms have value-capturing capabilities that perhaps have never been seen before. It is the extreme effectiveness of technology platforms as a business that opens up the possibility of extreme value capture. With so much value being concentrated in a few places—unless there are deliberate strategies or mechanisms to share wealth more broadly—increased wealth concentration is a likely result.

As the technological school of inequality has emphasized, the digital world offers powerful new capabilities for creating and capturing value. There are the network effects that might keep us on Facebook because all our family and friends are already there. There are the superstar effects, which lead us to seek out our favorite products and content from around the world. There is the power of exclusive data, particularly about customers and their previous history of accepting or rejecting offers. But the power of these technological features manifests itself through the business model, or specific business practices of the major technology companies.

Features of the institutional context school also play a role. To the extent that equity ownership is highly unequal in society, the wealth concaptured by digital business models will tend to stay concentrated. With wealth concentrated in virtual assets such as intellectual property, technology companies are able to assign their assets, and their profits, to the most favorable and lowest tax regulatory regimes around the world. The unprecedented degree to which major technology companies have been able to amass giant cash stockpiles overseas is not a coincidence.

One of the most fundamental problems of entrepreneurship—how to capture value—has been solved to an unprecedented degree by digital platforms. But the problem may have been solved too well in the sense that major technology companies can create technological mediations, and fine-tune the business model, to precisely the parameters that keep every stakeholder group participating, but maximize the remaining value capture for themselves. Digital mediators, if they so choose, can pay everyone just enough to keep all parties in a business model playing, but no more than necessary. The value captured for themselves is then distributed according to their idiosyncratic situations and histories, but often in a way that reflects the values and the power of the parties they must mobilize for the business models to work.

9.3 Changing the Technological Roadmap

What does a focus on wealth shifts and business models imply for the technology itself? Are there specific technology directions to be encouraged, or discouraged, in order to reverse increases in wealth inequality?

We have used technological mediation as a concept to describe specific technology choices. According to technology mediation theory, digital technology makes a set of representational choices about two basic types of relationships: how people relate to the world around them, and how people relate to each other. These mediation choices affect the way people see the world by amplifying or reducing elements of it. The choices also affect action by inviting or inhibiting certain kinds of behaviors. While this short description makes technology seem like a tool, or an instrument that brings human intentions to life, technologies that are highly entrenched, with few or no alternatives, and deeply embedded in everyday life will be experienced as more of a force outside of our control.

More nuanced approaches to studying technology mediation come from three additional philosophical positions on technological impact: 'history,' 'values' and 'practice.' History highlights previous commitments such as design, infrastructure, skills, and familiarity that give technology a trajectory or momentum that is difficult to change (Hughes 1987). Values imply some disagreement about which perceptions and actions should be encouraged by mediating technology. Practice emphasizes that technological mediation depends on multiple strands of persistent human activity that are shaped by tradition, and by the potential disconnects between what humans are trying to achieve in the world, and what they are actually able to do.

Both search and social media have evolved toward a complex mediation based on secretive algorithms driven by a business model that depends on selling access to an audience via advertising. These new digital technologies convey an image of neutrality, despite their lack of transparency. But their business model financially rewards constant experimentation with new forms of mediation that will increase usage and engagement, and only the platform owners themselves have access to the exclusive data and the code necessary to experiment with new business models, or variants of their existing business models, and to increase the amount of attention devoted to these systems. These unique capabilities help to concentrate financial wealth in the hands of the technology sector. Short of massive government interventions, on the level of the European Union or the US federal government, the data and code of technological mediations are not being shared.

Given the complexity of mediation, we have to ask what alternative technological mediations would look like—ones that might have fewer wealth-concentrating effects. Some commentators have focused on increasing the transparency of how technology works, and that is a positive step (Diakopoulos 2016). There is a role for educating people about the algorithms behind these platforms, and how they work. But there is also a role for building simpler platforms that are easier to understand. Less complex mediations, tied to less demanding business models, could give a wider range of people more of a choice about how these algorithms work.

It may seem unrealistic to try to compete with some of the wealthiest companies the world has even known, but there are digital capabilities that favor the Davids of the world over the Goliaths. One source of optimism will come from the recognition that the most important use cases for technology are fairly simple. If we look across the larger platforms, such as the web or social media, there are only a few basic types of relationships that will form the bulk of technology mediation. These use cases could either be recreated in entirely new platforms, or they could integrate with and extend existing platforms. We call these the three basic use cases of the digitally mediated economy: buyer-seller, person-person, and person-world.

The most important use case in our mediated market economy from a wealth concentration perspective is the connection between buyers and sellers, or between businesses and potential clients. At its most fundamental, what needs to be done is fairly simple. Businesses need to get offers in front of likely customers, and customers need to be able to find these offers and evaluate them. These functions do not require mediation through complex algorithms, particularly if businesses and consumers were offered more of a say in how their own searches worked and which messages from potential sellers they would or would not see. On alternative platforms, people might be able to express their own preferences rather than rely on a system that optimizes a business model, or use defaults that either come from organizations or peers they trust. There is much scope, and much need, for alternative mediations of the buyer-seller relationship, but little work is being done in this area. We are left with the implicit assumption that current technology industry business practices will lead us to the most effective solution. This may be true from a business model profit-maximization perspective, but not necessarily from a wealth-distribution perspective.

A second important use case is person-to-person relationships, as experienced most forcefully on social media. Though social media clearly engages people on a massive scale, with a reach of billions, the basic functionality the technology provides is not complicated. People need to subscribe to the updates, photos, and interesting content. They need to share comments. And they need to be able to like or otherwise vote on new content. A complex platform with secretive algorithms is not required for this. People could have the ability to control what they see by being able to tune or train their own algorithms, if the technological mediations can be built in a way that would not be too overwhelming. Giving the social media business model control over what people see for hours a day is centralizing too much value creation, and capture, in the companies that run the large technology platforms.

The third important use case is the person-to-world relationship identified by mediation theory. How do people understand what is happening in the world? The news people see is one highly relevant recent example, while, at the most abstract level, technology-based education could also be included as a mediated person-world relationship. A simpler platform could give people more control over their own destiny rather than assuming a large platform such as Facebook will naturally work toward the one perfect news source for everyone. Centralizing around a secretive set of algorithms is, again, allowing too much concentration of value creation and capture in one entity. By keeping the platform simpler, there exists the potential for alternatives that give people more control over what they see about the world on a daily basis.

Can more open technology be the solution to these problems? Further developing the capabilities of open technology certainly makes it easier to replace or extend existing technology platforms. Commentators such as Mason see open technologies, created and maintained outside of commercial considerations, as the solution to corporate algorithmic control (Mason 2016), and we share his enthusiasm. Powerful open technologies can get more technologists closer to creating solutions to these three basic use cases, reducing the amount of energy needed to mobilize groups to create an alternative. So far, however, alternative mediations have not made much of an impact and it remains a theoretical argument. But we do see platforms, such as Craigslist, that are able to scale up to hundreds of millions of users using simpler, widely available technologies and alternative business models.

Technology mediations that might decrease inequality are those that distribute the power to make decisions about who sees what and who connects to whom more broadly. Existing technology platforms will continue to claim a kind of neutrality and a commitment to ease of use and 'better' results, but the alleged neutrality of these major platforms must be challenged, not because non-neutrality is morally wrong, but because non-neutrality is unavoidable. Technology is a mediator of reality. It shapes human perception and action. It sometimes feels like an outside force, but it is not simply a force we can react to. Technology reflects very specific decisions, often made today on the basis of a commercial entity trying to satisfy their diverse constituents and keep a particular business model alive.

9.4 Changing the Model: Sharing Value with Its Creators

One of the main messages of this investigation is the need to consider business practices to understand technology's role in inequality. We argue that previous schools of thought about technology and inequality, the technological and the institutional context schools, are neglecting the influence of the business models used to deploy, govern, and further develop digital technology.

These business practices are not inevitable. The elements of the business model work together to determine how value is created, including technologies, resources, relationships, and the cooperation of multiple stakeholders in creating that value. Once that value is created, the business model also determines value. But how does each of the parties share in the value created?

We argue that digital technology has enabled companies in the technology sector to become incredibly skilled at discovering new ways to make money and to optimize the amount of profits earned. Digital technology increasingly mediates the most important economic relationships, especially the connection between buyers and sellers. But it is also the technological mediation of person-to-person relationships that affects economic behavior. Technology platforms also increasingly mediate the understanding we have of the world. Technology platforms shape the news we see, and the basic information and education we receive about all aspects of our world.

The business models that have developed around digital technologies are powerful, but also have a great potential for wealth concentration because their unique advantages are highly complex, opaque, and therefore not easily subject to outside scrutiny. The new business models tend to keep exclusive data for their own use in experimentation and optimization rather than selling it to third parties. By keeping this exclusive data for themselves, as well as the algorithms used to determine what people see, the new business models turn the classic functions of markets into a money-making opportunity for the companies controlling major technology platforms. Connections between people, including both commercial and personal relationships, are being shaped by a business model that depends on secrecy and exclusive ownership of data. A business model based on selling attention is potentially worrisome when these same platforms also mediate all the most important human relationships because the entity in the middle of these relationships uses a business model that encourages it to maximize its own value.

Even if these technology-induced business practices do create value, and have a tendency to concentrate that value in a few companies, there is nothing inevitable about how this value is shared with all the parties contributing to it. Is there some cultural factor built into the ethos of technology companies that might make them more likely to choose a different set of values from the prevailing corporate governance norms of shareholder wealth maximization, values that might make them want to share the benefits of this new economy more broadly? Companies such as Apple were born in an era of countercultural hacking and personal computing values, others like Google, also born in the same area, were formed with slogans such as 'Do No Evil,' and pledged to be different kinds of companies. As time progressed, the largest technology companies have behaved increasingly like other large modern corporations by maximizing shareholder value, awarding large amounts of equity- based executive compensation, and approving massive stock buyback programs to funnel that wealth to shareholders. There isn't much evidence that large technology companies have been more philanthropic to their communities than other comparable companies[1].

No matter how many individual coders or engineers might share anti-corporate values, examples of technology companies pursuing alternative values besides wealth maximization have been few and far between. The early stage funders of high-growth technology companies, such as seed investors, angels, and venture capitalists, are noteworthy for their investment return maximization outlook. As the interests of founders and managers are linked to those of high-risk investors through mechanisms such as stock option compensation, their business models pay even more attention to the wealth returned to these parties. Even the newer players—the technology startups who could theoretically shake up this order and distribute the gains more widely—are increasingly founded from the start to be acquired by one of the large technology companies in exchange for a massive payday for a core group of founders. The Facebooks, Alphabets, Apples, and Microsofts of the world are company-acquiring machines, able to use their equity and cash wealth stockpiles to buy any emerging companies which might offer an alternative.

Other than changes in skills and economic rules, we would propose two other places to look for solutions. First, we suggest actively searching for alternative business models in a digitally mediated world.

We need to focus on new business models, not just new technologies because, as we know, technology creates its main wealth-shifting effects through the business practices that create and capture value.

What we are aiming for could be described as a kind of 'markets.org.' Particularly for connecting buyers and sellers, we need to find more social enterprise-type business models for the three basic use cases along the lines of a Craigslist model for market discovery and transactions. In these alternative models, enough revenue is generated to keep the service going, and more value is shared with other parties as opposed to maximizing its own exclusive value and profits. As a more extreme alternative, a community-governed non-profit, or donations-based model, could redistribute the wealth.

But how realistic is it to search for new business models? It is easy to argue against, given the lack of successful alternative models to date. There are few examples of business models for explicitly social enterprises that have grown to be large technology companies. The pressures, the cultural expectations, and the temptations to further concentrate wealth are great. We can only hope that the connection between technology business models and inequality made more explicit will inspire some—possibly among this small group of wealthy technologists who might have concerns about rising inequality—to experiment with new solutions.

An encouraging sign for alternative business models is the underlying simplicity of the main use cases. Does it require sophisticated digital technology to share an advertisement? To share pictures with family and friends? Without the need to constantly optimize the business of attention, engagement, and transactions, these business operations could be much simpler. The technology infrastructure exists to experiment and scale new options quickly and cheaply. Just as existing platforms often start with concentrated audiences to build critical mass, so, too, could the alternative platforms start with concentrated populations on their own, or as a supplement to an existing platform.

The concept of mobilization provides another place to search for solutions. The major technology platforms that have so much wealth-generating power depend on complicated business models that require the ongoing mobilization, or active cooperation, of a diversity of interests. As we have seen with previous technological history and social movements, keeping consumers, providers, investors, advertisers, regulators, and community members all on board with a particular way to create and capture value is a highly complex task. Technology companies, because they can experiment with and optimize these arrangements to an unprecedented degree, offer just enough value to other parties to keep them cooperating, a dynamic that might also make their business models more sensitive to changes in what each party is willing to accept.

Can other stakeholders, such as consumers sharing their personal information, learn how to effectively demand more value for themselves? Can they develop more power to insist that these technologies better serve their own interests first? There is clearly room for this because the technology platform companies are capturing tremendous value based on basic services that are relatively cheaply provided at scale. Movements have not been able to coalesce around issues such as consumer privacy, or the organizing of ride-sharing drivers, but the recent example of consumers deleting Uber apps in favor of Lyft due to perceived political alliances might hold a clue to the power of user mobilization in the future (Kosoff 2017). Much attention has been focused on regulators, but technology companies have proven successful in keeping regulators sufficiently cooperative to give them the freedom to maneuver when they need to find and optimize business models. It may be that focusing on other value providers, such as consumers and service providers, could have a marginal impact on what technology platform companies might be more sensitive to.

Whatever the mechanism, the value capture equation has to be changed in order to address the inequality issue. The value created has to be shared more broadly, and for that to happen the business practices surrounding the technology will likely have to change.

9.5 Summing up: Technology and Inequality

The larger question remains: does technology drive inequality? It is a question that haunts this debate, and has motivated this investigation of where information technology might have gone astray. For those brought up in the eras of personal computing, or the first flowering of the Internet, severe economic inequality would be an ironic and disappointing outcome. Technology that puts more information in more hands than ever before should be an instrument of liberation and empowerment, not one of putting wealth and power in fewer hands.

A relationship between two large concepts like technology and inequality is bound to be a complex one. We began by reviewing the arguments for how and why technology might be implicated in the increasingly severe economic inequality found in technology-intensive developed economies. We identified two schools of thought, the technological, which argues that inherent features of new technology lead to the concentration of wealth and power, and institutional context, which argues that technology plays a lesser or supporting role in growing economic inequality when compared to the economic game of taxation policies, intellectual property rules, and other features of the institutional environment.

Both schools are limited in terms of solutions. From the technological school of explanation, we inherit the logic that technology acts as a force of nature that can only be adapted to, not shaped by human choices and commitments. We can increase education and skill levels, but the fundamental response is to adjust to a reality beyond our control. Institutional context might suggest a number of adjustments to the economic rules of the game, such as taxation policy, corporate governance, or intellectual property protection These could be useful suggestions, but depend on an appetite and capacity for political change across national boundaries that are difficult to find.

What we have tried to do, instead, is find new, previously neglected aspects of the technology and inequality story to highlight concepts that could bring us closer to specific processes of wealth concentration and reveal new kinds of solutions. First, we focus on wealth as the key measure of inequality and power, the characteristics of which have shifted in the US, in particular, since 1980, which saw assets moving from real property to financial instruments, and the value of large corporate equity dramatically moving from the energy and commodities sectors to information technology and finance. Information technology companies have amassed unprecedented cash piles, and have been channeling this wealth to their shareholders, already among the wealthiest households, at a furious rate. The amount of wealth shift in the US alone is in the trillions of dollars, enough to explain a reasonable fraction of growing wealth inequality.

The shift to financial assets, and the rise in value and profits of the information technology and finance sectors, point to what might be called the 'rise of the virtualized economy.' These two sectors are no longer limited to assisting the 'real' economy; they have become the real economy where, increasingly, products and services are created and delivered digitally. At the same time, the basic functions of market economies, such as discovering and choosing a business to buy from, are digitally mediated. Buyers and sellers are being connected through complex, non-transparent digital platforms controlled by massive corporations.

To understand this shift, we need to understand the business models of the digital platform companies that have become powerful enough to shift wealth so significantly. The business model describes how a particular platform creates value, and how the value created is captured and shared with other parties whose active cooperation is essential. As many an entrepreneur has learned, simply inventing something new or making something better does not guarantee the benefits of that invention will accrue to the inventor. Value has to be captured. A business model has to be built around it. For many entrepreneurs, finding a value capture method that works is a real problem.

In the new digital world, we argue, these large technology companies have solved the value capture problem—with a vengeance. Through constant experimentation, uniquely owned and controlled data sets, and an ability to quickly and cheaply scale up to millions or even billions, digital technology companies can experiment with new business models, extending business models to new industries, recombining them, and varying the details within them to the extent that they control exactly how value is shared, in turn creating a digitally mediated world where the most important economic relationships increasingly operate through their technology-fueled business practices.

The potential profitability of new digital business models has, of course, been celebrated in business research. But optimizing digital business model technology also seems to concentrate wealth. To understand technology and inequality, we need to look carefully at the digitally mediated world we already exist in, not just speculate about artificial intelligence in the future.

Left to their own devices, the technology sector can concentrate wealth if they so desire. There are complex combinations of desires and goals at these technology companies, but the institutional context of their businesses, particularly their links to high-risk investing and finance, are too strong for those desires to be consistently resisted without sustained and concerted effort. New digital platforms will have to be shaped by new values in general, and new business models specifically, to truly shift the technology and inequality relationship toward reducing inequality rather than reinforcing it.

For this to happen, there will have to be changes in the value model, or how value is captured and shared. Our framework points to two ways in which digital business models are implemented: through mediating relationships digitally, and through mobilizing a diversity of parties, motivating them to continue participating in a business model. On the mediation side, we have identified the three major use cases, or relationships represented in this new economy: buyer-to-seller, person-to-person, and person-to-world. The technology infrastructure to create alternative solutions, driven by more equitable business models, is improving all the time, thanks to cloud infrastructure and all manner of open technology. The technological ability to implement alternative models is there, assuming that their corresponding business models do not depend on complexity and secrecy. Though industries like search, social, and sharing have precisely tuned themselves to provide convenience, functionality, and just enough value for all parties to keep everyone at the table, the core functionality they provide can be replicated. With enough push, or even just the slow decline of reputation over time, other alternatives can take their place. Giving people more control over the methods and algorithms used to mediate these relationships is an excellent start, but one that is difficult to achieve if the basic business model is not changed.

The other path to change is to mobilize various interest groups in ways that make them more conscious of the value they are contributing to these business models, and more insistent on capturing or sharing that value for and with themselves. Much of the attention focuses on the regulators and giving them more leverage in cases such as the sharing economy, which has made an impact. But the choices should not end there. An underexplored and more speculative option would be to make end-user consumers more aware of their value, and more willing to assert their demands by, for example, partially or completely withdrawing from certain platform uses. Another unexplored constituency are the technology coders and designers. Can they be infused with a new vision, a new willingness to provide these fundamental services in a different way?

To crack the technology and inequality problem, we need to think more in terms of business models, and how to implement new ones. It is not just a matter of more education or better regulations, though both would help. There are very specific business practices having a disproportionate impact on wealth inequality, and therefore global opportunity. Arguments about technology and society have usually underplayed the role of business practices and investors, focusing more on inventors, users, and politicians. This needs to change.

In sum, we argue that specific technology-fueled business practices have, so far, encouraged wealth concentration. Established players have a number of technology-related advantages that are difficult to overcome. Theoretically, technology should not be an inevitable force of inequality, but it has been in practice. Finding and implementing new models must be made an explicit priority; change will not happen naturally on its own.

Obviously, there is no single magic solution, and there aren't yet enough good role models to follow or expand upon. More experimentation with new business models and more trials are needed. It may be more effective to scan the horizon for early experiments that show promising signs, and helping them to scale, instead of forcing existing systems to change, or inventing completely new substitutes all at once.

Our focus on technology and inequality is perhaps an unpleasant story of power reinforcement and entrenchment instead of the usual discourse about technology's power for radical revolution, creative destruction, or disruptive innovation. We do not deny the power of technology to change the world. Far from it. Only that it does not always change the world as we would hope. It should not be this way, and—more importantly—does not have to be this way. Technology can do better.

Note

1. Large technology companies seem to be underrepresented on the list of the top 20 most philanthropic organizations, see (Preston 2016).

References

Anand, S., & Sen, A. (1994). Human development index: Methodology and measurement. Retrieved February 21, 2017, from http://hdr.undp.org/en/content/human-development-index-methodology-and-measurement.

Breen, R. (Ed.). (2004). *Social mobility in Europe*. Oxford, UK: Oxford University Press.

Diakopoulos, N. (2016). Accountability in algorithmic decision making. *Communications of the ACM, 59*(2), 56–62.

Hughes, T. P. (1987). The evolution of large technological systems. In W. E. Bijker, T. P. Hughes, & T. J. Pinch (Eds.), *The social construction of technological systems: New directions in the sociology and history of technology* (pp. 51–82). Cambridge, MA: MIT Press.

Kosoff, M. (2017). How the #deleteUber campaign revealed Uber's fatal flaw. http://www.vanityfair.com/news/2017/02/how-the-deleteuber-campaign-revealed-ubers-fatal-flaw.

Mason, P. (2016). *Postcapitalism: A guide to our future*. New York: Farrar, Straus and Giroux.

Preston, C. (2016). The 20 most generous companies of the fortune 500. Retrieved February 22, 2017, from http://fortune.com/2016/06/22/fortune-500-most-charitable-companies/.

Sen, A. (1999). *Development as freedom*. New York: Oxford University Press.

Shane, S. A. (2003). *A general theory of entrepreneurship: The individual-opportunity nexus*. Cheltenham: Edward Elgar.

Index

A
Actor network theory, 83
Advertising business model, 52, 97, 104, 112, 117
Airbnb, 32, 36, 50, 67, 69, 90, 122–124, 126, 128–132
Algorithms
  non-transparent, 2
  secret, or secretive, 43, 52, 93, 113, 140, 143, 145
Alphabet, 35, 48, 102, 147
Amazon, 32, 47, 48, 50, 53, 67, 69, 80, 89, 101, 103, 104
Android operating system, 15, 98
Angel investors, 5, 32, 99, 147
Apple, 3, 16, 17, 30, 31, 33, 36, 48, 50, 63, 67, 68, 79, 80, 88, 89, 147
Artificial intelligence, 3, 18, 33, 99, 139, 151
Automation, 1, 5, 7, 13, 14, 18, 39, 71, 139

B
Benkler, Y., 19, 62, 65

Big data, 18, 34, 52, 139
Buybacks, share, 30

C
Cloud computing, 38, 50
Complementary assets, 34
Conversion rate, 53, 100, 101
Copyright, 34, 62, 64, 65
Corporate governance, 1, 147, 150
Craigslist, 50, 51, 79, 145, 148
Customer value proposition, 78, 79, 87, 88, 126

D
Differential voting rights, shares with, 48
Digital Millennium Copyright Act, 64

E
Engine of opportunity, technology as, 1, 137, 138, 140
Eras of digital technology
  mainframe era, 3, 5, 14
  personal computing era, 3, 5, 33

Exclusive data, 43, 52, 57, 141, 146
Experimentation, 2, 19, 37, 56, 114, 126, 143, 151

F
Facebook, 30, 31, 35, 38, 50, 52, 55, 80, 101, 104, 108–116, 145
Financialization, 26, 139
Frictionless market, 45, 49

G
Gini coefficients, 11, 25
Globalization, 7, 14, 72
Google, 35, 47, 48, 54, 55, 80, 95–103

H
Hypothesis, business model, 35, 78, 79

I
Inequality
  ethnic, 11, 12, 27
  income, 7, 10, 11, 13, 17, 25, 66
  wealth, 2, 10, 11, 13, 25, 38, 57, 72, 139, 140, 150, 152
Information asymmetries, 2, 44, 46, 123
Infrastructure
  cloud, 38, 80, 81, 152
  digital, 11, 37, 71, 72
  technology, 17, 37, 38, 108, 148, 152
Instagram, 30, 38, 110
Institutional context school, 3, 16, 17, 19, 31, 66, 72, 73, 77, 82, 137
Intangible assets, 61, 67
Intellectual property
  assets, 31, 63, 67

law, 2, 16, 19, 69
  protection, 34, 62, 65, 150
Investors, mobilizing, 86, 99, 116, 127, 152

L
Levy, S., 97
LinkedIn, 36, 108, 116, 117
Lobbying, political, 61, 68
Lyft, 69, 123, 124, 128, 130, 149

M
Market capitalization, 29, 102, 140
Markets
  digitally mediated, 48, 50, 140
  perfect, 6, 44, 47, 52, 54, 140
  two-sided, 87, 122, 126–128
Mason, P., 18, 27, 145
Mediation theory, technological action choices, 84
  coercive, 85
  decisive, 85
  force of influence, 85
  multistability, 85
  perception choices, 84
  persuasive, 85
  seductive, 85
  visibility of influence, 85
Microsoft, 15, 36, 68, 80, 88, 89, 102, 117, 147
Middle class, 10, 138
Mobilization, technology, 3, 77, 86, 87, 93, 104, 121, 137
Monopoly, 16, 45, 55, 62, 64
MySpace, 110, 114

N
Negative externalities, 44
Netflix, 36, 37, 50, 141

New economy, 6, 147, 152
News feed, social media, 55, 85, 108, 110–112, 117

O
Open source software, 5, 46
Open technology, 18, 65, 145, 152
Oxfam, 7, 10

P
Patent
  portfolio, 63
  software, 62, 63
Peer production, 65
Piketty, T., 8, 10, 19, 25, 138
Practical freedom, 11, 138
Profile, social media, 108, 109, 112
Purchasing decisions, online, 97, 103

R
Regulations
  financial, 16
  institutional, 72
  privacy, 69, 101
Regulators, mobilizing, 87, 95, 101, 103, 115, 128, 129, 148, 152
Regulatory arbitrage, 2, 72
Reich, R., 14
Rent-seeking, 45
Representational choices, 94, 142

S
Scalability, 25, 37, 38, 141
Search costs, 45, 46, 49
Search engine optimization, 54, 56, 95, 110
Sen, A., 11
Skills-biased technological change, 14

Small and medium-sized enterprises, 32
Social construction of technology, 83
Social media use, effects of, 110
S&P 500, 32, 61
Stiglitz, J., 10, 17, 27, 43, 47, 138
Stock options, 31, 32
Subscription business model, 35–37
Superstar effects, 39, 141
Surveillance, 52, 69, 70

T
Taxation policy, 31, 66, 150
Tax avoidance, 17, 31, 66, 67, 103
Technological determinism, 4, 15, 82
Technological school, 13, 14, 17, 18, 29, 82, 141, 150
Technology as
  force, 82, 83
  history, 2, 82, 83, 85, 148
  practice, 83
  tool, 2, 139
  values, 83, 143
Teece, D., 33–35, 79
Twitter, 36, 114, 116

U
Uber, 36, 69, 70, 87, 122–124, 126, 128–130
Unique data, 2, 49, 99, 132, 140

V
Value capture, 33, 34, 37, 52, 70, 88, 96, 103, 104, 118, 125, 141, 149, 151
Value creation, 33, 35, 77, 81, 88, 96, 118, 141, 144, 145
Venture capital, 5, 12, 56, 70, 99, 128
Virtualized economy, 2, 29, 140, 150

W
Wages, 31, 88, 102, 117, 129
Wealth concentration, 25, 29, 32, 38, 39, 61, 63, 90, 102, 103, 117, 144, 146, 150, 153
Wealth shift, 6, 28, 29, 39, 88, 89, 116, 137, 139–142, 150
WhatsApp, 30, 117

Wikipedia, 65
Winner-take-all effects, 2, 116

Y
Yahoo!, 70, 94, 98
YouTube, 50, 64, 90, 96, 98, 99

The manufacturer's authorised representative in the EU is Springer Nature Customer Service Centre GmbH, Europaplatz 3, 69115 Heidelberg, Germany. If you have any concerns regarding our products, please contact ProductSafety@springernature.com

Printed and bound by CPI Group (UK) Ltd, Croydon, CR0 4YY
23/03/2026
02076447-0014